EYEWITNESS
TO
HEAVEN

a glimpse into the obscure

EYEWITNESS
TO
HEAVEN

james wilburn chauncey

a memoir

TATE PUBLISHING & *Enterprises*

Published by Tate Publishing & Enterprises, LLC
127 E. Trade Center Terrace | Mustang, Oklahoma 73064 USA
1.888.361.9473 | www.tatepublishing.com

Tate Publishing is committed to excellence in the publishing industry. The company reflects the philosophy established by the founders, based on Psalm 68:11,
"The Lord gave the word and great was the company of those who published it."

Book design copyright © 2011 by Tate Publishing, LLC. All rights reserved.
Cover design by Sarah Kirchen
Interior design by Nathan Harmony

Published in the United States of America

ISBN: 978-1-61346-013-9
Biography & Autobiography / Personal Memoirs
11.10.06

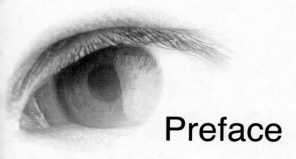

Preface

How many times have you said to yourself, "I wish I knew what is going to happen tomorrow" or something similar? Actually, do you think knowing what is going to happen would be advantageous to you? Many, I think, would love to know what is going to happen tomorrow or next week or next year or even ten years from now so they can profit by the knowledge. What if you knew that although you can very well profit by that knowledge, you also knew that the final outcome would be unpleasant? Suppose you knew that in the end all your profiting would be for naught. So I ask this: if I knew things in the future were going to rapidly deteriorate into a painful ordeal for my family, my friends, and country, what should I tell them, or what should I do? Now think of the burden that would place upon you. This is the burden I have carried for more than six decades.

The political atmosphere around the world is fueled by religious opinions. On the one side is pro-religion representing many religious orders, and on the other side is the anti-religion. Each side is becoming more outspoken and more dogmatic or fanatical about their position than has been seen for centuries or even millennia. Nevertheless, the most dangerous of all is the strife that exists within each group. This book isn't about any pro or anti-religious groups, but it is an account of what happened between heaven and me at the age of seven when I died, three weeks before turning eight years of age.

Religion and righteousness aren't, I repeat, aren't the same.

As my dad always said, "Son, the proof of the pudding is in the eating, not the talking about it."

It is the interpretation of religious information that is the problem. Nevertheless, this book isn't about religion; it is about—well, form your own opinion. I hope that the reading of this book will prove beneficial. Nevertheless, with some I know the label "kook," "crazy," "ignorant fool," and so forth will attach itself to me.

Over the past few months, the conviction that heaven wants my experiences made known has become more and more apparent. My choice for six decades has been to never talk or write about the experiences. I am under great stressful pain thinking about the possibilities of persecution that may be heaped upon my family. Because of this pain, on many occasions, I have repeatedly asked God to remove this burden from me. His answer is always the same: "Remember Nineveh."

Some of what you will read aren't my words. They are words that have appeared in my mind, and I have written them here for you to read.

Table of Contents

How I Died

The majority of the first seven years of my life was as normal as was any little boy's are. That is, if you can attribute normality to any little boy. The thing that stands out about me as a little boy is from a comment my mother would make from time to time. If I were anything then like my two grandsons are now, I have no doubt she made the comment in frustration from having to put up with my shenanigans.

She would say to me, "Wilburn, you can start a fight just by walking into a room."

For years that bothered me, so one day when I was about forty-five years old, I got up the courage to ask her what she meant, and if I was so bad. She said that basically I was a good kid but so inquisitive and argumentative about everything that when I walked into a room, I began questioning everybody about everything that had been said, and that upset everyone. I suppose that unseemly and unpopular quality, or maybe it wasn't a quality at all, would play a big part in the ordeal that was about to befall seven-year-old me, three weeks before my eighth birthday.

One evening after supper, I was playing in the front yard at our old home on Walden's Ridge in Tennessee, in the small community of Fairmount. The house was about nine hundred square feet and sat on a little less than two thirds of an acre. Eight people lived in the house. There was Mom, Dad, my three older brothers, my older sister, my younger brother, and me. To say the least, it was a bit crowded, but we all got along as well as most other families, maybe a little better than some and maybe a little worse than some others. As a family we grew most of our own food and took care of ourselves without any help from anyone, especially any government. Self-reliance, fairness to all, and "your word is your bond" were the codes my family lived by and practiced.

That evening, my sister, Earlene, came to me and stood there with her hands on her hips for a moment before she spoke. Sister grew up with five brothers, and she had no problem holding her own.

Dad had instilled in all of us boys to always, "Treat your sister with respect just as you do your mother, and don't ever let me catch you pushing her around."

I am sorry to say those instructions only went so far. Sometime we were all guilty of popping Sister a time or two, but when Mom or Dad caught us, it was hell to pay. She was a very serious girl with a true loving and caring about her that isn't found in many people.

Sister said, "I want you to go to the revival with me tonight. It is your turn."

"What's a revival?" I asked.

"It is where a man of God tries to get everyone saved, and you need saving," she answered.

"Saved from what?" I asked.

"Don't ask so many questions. Just get up, and let's go," she insisted.

"No," I said.

It was easy to tell she was getting aggravated with me, and I knew from experience I didn't want to aggravate her very much.

"Look! Last night I took your twin brothers, but they refuse to go with me tonight, so you will go with me whether you want to or not."

"But I don't want to go."

Sternly, almost ordering me, she said, "Come on. Get up. You're going with me and that's it."

I always loved to argue, which often got me in trouble, so I said, "What makes you think you can order me around?"

"Listen, I'm the only sister; it's my duty to see to it that all my brothers have been saved. That's what Grandma told me to do, so get up, brush the dirt off, wash up, and Dad will take us to the revival."

"Okay." I went into the house, got cleaned up, and we went.

Dad drove us to the revival in our 1941 Packard. Sister made me sit up close to the front of the tent near the podium. I squirmed around a bit, but I made it through the service. The revival service was boring, and I couldn't wait until it was over and I could go home. Dad picked us up, but as far as the revival was concerned, I figured I never had to go again.

Now don't get me wrong, even though Mother and Dad grew up in stringently religious families, our family wasn't what you would call every-Sunday-go-to-meeting religious. I suppose we were about as ordinary of a family as a mountain family could be in the mid-1940s. Mom was a homemaker, and Dad was a school bus driver, and of course, he was the farmer in the family. We raised almost all the vegetables, fruits, and meats on our table.

The next evening I was outside playing because it was summer, there was no homework to be done, and all of our chores were completed. We didn't have a lot of toys. Most of the toys we had were make-believe toys from blocks of wood and things we made ourselves. I was playing with such a toy, calling them my cars, when I heard a voice saying it was time to go. Looking around to see who was talking to me, I saw no one. My first thought was that it was my dad, but he was nowhere in sight; neither was anyone else. Not seeing anyone, I returned to playing, and again I heard the voice: "You need to get up and go now."

I looked around, and there was no one there, so I went back to playing. This time the voice was much louder and sterner.

"What!" I responded.

Once again I looked around for the voice when I heard, "You need to get up now and go to the tent revival on the highway."

The voice was so stern. This time I paid attention, got up, dusted the dirt off my overalls, and without saying anything to anyone, I headed down the driveway. Reaching the road, I looked over my shoulder just as I heard Sister, standing on the front porch, hollering, "Supper's ready. Come on and eat, y'all."

Stopping, I turned around and started walking toward the house, and then I stopped, turned my head and looked at the road. Slowly, I started toward the road without supper. I walked barefooted all the way, about a mile, to the tent revival.

The sun was about to go down when I finally got there. Hot, sweaty, with feet hurting, an usher looked at my dirty overalls and bare feet and greeted me with a puzzled look on his face. Taking me by the hand, he escorted me to the back row of benches. Placing his Bible and songbook on the bench, he helped me up onto his Bible and songbook, making it possible for me to see over the adults sitting in front of me. The night before I couldn't wait for the service to be over, but here I was again tonight. I couldn't help listening intently as the preacher talked about where a person goes when they die. Then he asked, "If you should die tonight, where will you spend eternity?"

I pondered this question for a moment then accepted his invitation to come to the front and talk to him about it.

As I reached the front of the tent, he looked at me and stepped down from the pulpit to greet me. Taking me by the hand, he introduced himself as Pastor Lee Roberson.

"It is always wonderful to see a young person like yourself make their way down to be saved... Are your parents here?" he inquired.

"No, I came by myself."

Leading me to the front row pew, he knelt in front of me. We read scripture together, and while talking, he explained Jesus to me in a way no one had ever explained. That night I felt Jesus come into my heart, and I was no longer afraid. He took me by the hand as he was ending the service and introduced me to the congregation, and I stayed with him at the front of the tent until almost everyone departed.

With the tent almost empty, I walked to the edge of the highway, hoping Dad would figure out where I was and come get me. As the last car left the tent site, I figured Dad wasn't coming, so I crossed the road and headed toward home. When I reached the other side of the road, I paused and looked back at the tent. Then it hit me. I was by myself. Now I had to walk the lonely dark country road, without streetlights, all the way home.

It was a cloudy night, so the moon didn't light the road. Cautiously, I began to walk, as I kept telling myself that I had been down these roads many times before so I shouldn't be afraid. Even if I couldn't see the road, I could tell when I was about to go into the ditch by feeling the gravels along the side of the road with my bare feet. I made my way down the dark road, occasionally looking up toward heaven asking God to protect me. After walking for about ten minutes, I stepped on loose gravel in front of me, and I knew instinctively that I needed to turn right at that intersection. Even though I continually wished a car would come along, none did. It was impossible for me to see where I was going, but soon I heard water running from the creek a little ahead of me across the Colby property where I crossed a wooden bridge. There were no guardrails on the side of the bridge, so I had to be very careful or I might have fallen off the bridge into the water. Making it across the bridge, I started up the small incline at the curve in the road where my eldest brother had been killed by a drunk driver about fifteen years earlier.

It was early spring when one evening Mom was working in the flower garden close to the property line near the road when a drunk driver came around the bend in the road, jumped the ditch, barely missing Mom by inches, and hit the basket in which Mom and Dad's first-born son was sleeping. Mom didn't want to leave Ralph, the first born, in the house or on the porch alone, so she had wrapped him in a blanket and put him in a basket to have him near her while she worked so she could look after him. Moms are like that, especially with their first born. The doctors couldn't find anything wrong with the baby, but after the accident, he just couldn't breathe well. Within a few weeks, the baby died, having devastating effects on Mom and Dad. The accident, and that is all it was, could never be fully accepted by either of them. Three years later they would lose two other babies—twins. As newly weds and new parents losing three infant children took its toll on them and often created violent arguments over things trivial. However, God would bless Mom and Dad with a second set of twins two and a half years later. It was the second set of twins that had gone to the revival with sister the previous day. Five short years after losing the first set of twins, my parents faced losing another child, me. Losing four of their nine children in fifteen years would have certainly torn the family apart. At the top of the hill and around the curve, it was a straight shot to the house, about a half a mile ahead. I began thinking, *I am going to make it,* when I saw a faint light ahead and realized my house wasn't far away.

Within about quarter of a mile of my house, the clouds parted, and for a few moments, the moon lit up the road. I had passed the house with the light, and I saw another light down the road. It was my house; I faintly heard people calling my name. Mom and Dad were firm believers in "spare the rod and spoil the child" so I thought, *Oh no, I'll bet I am in trouble now; they sound angry, really angry; I'm going to get it now.* Even knowing I was going to get into trouble, I walked faster and faster until I was almost running. Reaching the driveway, with my voice quivering a little, I hollered, "Here I am! Here I am."

Dad was the first to see me.

"Where have you been, boy? Our entire neighborhood has been out looking for you."

Mom, standing on the front steps, yelled, "There he is! There he is! Come here, son! Hurry! Hurry! Thank God, you're safe. You should be whipped good for scaring us like that, but I am so glad you are safe. All I want to do is hug you. Come on, I'll get you something to eat... You must be hungry since you missed supper."

The next day no one seemed to care about what happened the previous night except for Sister. When she asked what happened to me, I told her how I met Jesus Christ and how scary it was to walk home. She didn't seem too surprised at all at what happened with me.

Within a few days things had gone back to normal. The dog days of summer were in full swing. Two of my brothers and I were playing in the yard, and my sister was sitting on the front steps watching.

Late in the evening while riding my brother's bicycle, a terrible pain hit me in the back of the head at the base of my skull, as if someone had hit me with a ball bat or something. The pain hit so hard it knocked me unconscious, and both the bicycle and I took a tumble over a small swell in the yard. My sister and brothers, seeing the crash, came running to help.

When I regained consciousness, I found myself sitting on the sidewalk to our front porch. A headache was beginning to set in, so Sister helped me to the steps of the porch and sat with me until Mom called her in to set the table for supper. The headache was getting worse, so I went into the house to ask Mom for something to stop the pain. She gave me some aspirin and sent me back outside. Once there, I sat down on the steps, and as time passed, the headache didn't dissipate. Back into the house I went, asking Mom for something else to help with the pain. She searched and found some headache powders and gave them to me.

Dad came home from work, so Mom and Sister set the food on the table for supper. Normally I would be placed near the other end of the table, but Dad sat me next to him because my head was hurting so bad. After the food was served, Dad asked me why I wasn't eating. I told him my head hurt so much that I couldn't eat. He insisted I eat something, saying that eating would probably help make my headache go away. I took a couple of bites and spewed all over that end of the table. You can imagine the reaction from Dad and Sister, who were also sitting at the end of the table. Mom rushed me into the bathroom, cleaned me up, and took me back to the table. I refused to sit down, and as she was about to make me sit down, I spewed again. This time I was standing and able to direct it away from the table and toward the floor. By now my parents were beginning to take my pain seriously.

Vomiting came more often, so Mom put me to bed, but by now the pain was intense and traveling down my spine. The more water and aspirin they gave me, the more I vomited. It wasn't long until I was vomiting so often that Dad put a bucket beside my bed because there wasn't time to get me to the bathroom. Periods of unconsciousness began to set in, and when I regained consciousness, I would arch my back in pain. Mom later told me that she thought my back would break because I arched it so high. Dad called Dr. Hair, the same doctor who delivered me, to come quickly. Upon arrival and examination, Dr. Hair couldn't make a diagnosis because the spots he said looked similar to measles, but they were larger, and the other symptoms didn't match. He departed immediately for his office to look up the symptoms cautioning Dad to keep everyone away from me because I was probably highly contagious.

It didn't take long for him to call and tell Dad it appeared as though I had bacterial (Meningococcal) meningitis in the spine and brain, and death would come within a few short hours. He also told Dad not to worry because I would soon go unconscious and wouldn't recover, after which I would no longer feel any pain. Death should come within a couple hours or so after midnight. Dad would hear none of that and insisted on taking me to the children's hospital in Chattanooga. Dr. Hair told him that would be useless, that even if I managed to survive, all my brain function would be destroyed by the disease and high body temperatures and that the hospital would probably turn him away because of the infectiousness of the disease. Dad told Dr. Hair that he was leaving with me anyway to go to the hospital and asked him to please let the hospital know he was coming. Mom and Dad wrapped me up in a quilt, ran with me to the car, and sped off toward the hospital.

On the drive down the mountain to the hospital, Dad didn't let any grass grow underneath the wheels of our Packard. I continued to vomit, arch my back, hallucinate, and thrash about, and it was almost impossible for Mom to hold and control me in the backseat. My older brother Clyde was riding in the front seat with Dad leaning over the seat trying to help Mom control me. On the way I hallucinated about going off a bridge into the Tennessee River and about women's underwear and many other things. Somewhere along the way Dad was stopped by the police for speeding and when they saw me they gave us an escort to the hospital with sirens blaring and red lights flashing. When we arrived at the hospital, Dad ran first with me to the front door, but they wouldn't let him in and made him take me to the emergency entrance at the rear of the building where a medical team awaited my arrival.

In those days, anyone with bacterial meningitis had to be quarantined. When the hospital staff heard a highly contagious patient was being transported to them, they had no choice but to frantically empty a ward leaving only one bed and one table in the room. The moment I arrived at the emergency entrance the hospital staff placed me on a gurney, tied me with restraints, and covered my entire body with sheets as they ran with me to the quarantine room.

Bacterial (Meningococcal) spinal meningitis was one of the most feared and deadly diseases of the 1940s. More than 99 percent of those infected by the disease died within twelve hours of displaying the first symptoms. Of the less than 1 percent who survived the disease, the resulting high fever had such a devastating effect on the brain they developed into an almost helpless individual requiring total care to sustain their life.

Some refer to this as being as a living vegetable. That was to be my fate had I survived. The hospital staff struggled and struggled to restrain me, so much so that they had to bind my hands and feet to the head and footboard of the bed.

They made it to the hospital ward, and as they were working on me, it happened. All of the sudden, I came out of my body and could see the hospital staff working on me. When I came out of my body, it seemed as if I came out through my mouth or the top of my head. I could see everything as I stood erect in the air, maybe a foot above the floor. There was no pain, no discomfort, and I felt wonderful, at peace, and happy just watching the doctor and nurses. My body was lying on the hospital bed naked with my wrist and ankles tied to the headboard and footboard rails of the hospital bed with cloth strips and tape. It was amazing; I could see and hear everything they were saying to each other about me. When I looked at myself, I was amazed to see I was as tall as they were. *Impossible*, I thought, *I am only seven years old. How could I grow so quickly?* There was a metal table about three feet from the right side of the bed pushed up to the wall. Two IV poles with five IV bottles were standing to the left side of the bed. Tubes ran from the bottles to my arms and legs. There were three nurses and one doctor in the room. They were completely covered with white hospital gowns, masks, and head coverings. The doctor and one nurse were standing next to the right side of the bed and two nurses and IV poles to the left side.

The doctor asked the nurse standing next to him about my pulse, blood pressure, respiration, and temperature. She told him she could not detect a pulse; my temperature had fallen below ninety-six degrees, and there was only a faint sign of breathing. The doctor instructed the two nurses on the left to cover me with sheets and blankets in an attempt to keep me warm. One nurse asked the doctor if she could lay beside me in hopes she could pass some of her body heat to me. He told her it was no use, that nothing could help me now. The doctor told the nurse to the right to monitor me and that he would be right back. A few minutes later, the doctor returned and looked at the clipboard on the table, shook his head, and asked for an update on my vital signs. I thought the nurse was going to cry as she told the doctor she couldn't detect any vital signs and now there was no sign of breathing. The doctor hesitated a moment, looked toward the ward door, reluctantly recorded a time of death for me, and instructed the nurses to prepare my body for cremation in accordance with county ordinances.

Suddenly a man came through the outside wall of the hospital room. *Whoa!* I didn't believe or understand what I just saw.

"Who are you?" I asked. "And how did you do that?"

He told me that two angels had been sent to take me to paradise.

"What? You are going to take me where?"

"Paradise," the angel repeated. He continued, "You were very sick and your body died, and when a young person unexpectedly dies, angels are sent to take them to paradise."

"Why did I die?" I asked.

"Your time hadn't yet come, but you had a very bad illness," the angel responded.

"If it isn't my time to die, then why did I die?" I asked.

He told me that all people have a set time to die; however, other things can alter that time, such as sickness, accidents, and interferences of man.

"Where is the other angel?" I asked.

"The other angel is late for just that kind of reason." The angel told me an automobile accident had occurred and a young woman was killed, and since it wasn't her time to die, the other angel was escorting her to paradise.

"It will be a little while before the other angel returns; then we will all leave together."

After the doctor recorded my time of death, he turned to leave the room to speak with Mom and Dad. They had been waiting in the hall for hours to hear some good news. I wanted to follow the doctor into the corridor, but I couldn't get a grip on the doorknob. The angel asked me what I was trying to do. I told him I wanted to go out to see my parents. The angel took me by the hand and led me through the door into the corridor.

Mom and Dad were in tears. Mom could hardly stand she was so distraught. The doctor told Mom and Dad that everything possible that could be done had been done. Just as predicted, the meningitis was fatal, and they needed to go home, comfort the other children, and make preparations for a memorial service. They didn't like the idea of cremation at all, but there was nothing they could do about it because the County Health Department was now in control of my body, so there was nothing left for them to do except go home.

Devastated, they asked the doctor if it would be possible for them to go inside and say good-bye. Quickly, the angel and I went back through the wall into the room. My parents donned hospital gowns and masks and entered the room. Seeing the sorrow in them, I couldn't any longer contain myself, so I began shouting, "I'm here! I'm here," but they couldn't hear me. I reached out to hug Mom, but my arms passed right through her. I was screaming and crying as Mom and Dad leaned over my body, as if to kiss me good-bye.

I screamed to the angel that I wouldn't go with him. I couldn't stand to see them hurting so much. I tried again to put my arms around Mom. As my arms passed through her, I could barely feel the sensation. I began begging my parents, "Don't go! Don't go! Don't leave me here! I'm here!" I shouted repeatedly. All I could do was watch as my parents left the hospital ward. Mom was sobbing, "No, no, not again. I just can't take losing another baby; I can't bear it."

Begging and screaming that I wouldn't go with the angels didn't help matters. Seeing Mom and Dad leave the hospital ward and head down the corridor was the last time I thought I would ever see them. The angel calmed me by saying that they—the angels—couldn't make me go if I chose not to go, but I would be left in the hospital area, maybe for many generations. He said that if I refused to go that no one would know I was here. It would be as though I was a lost spirit.

The angel took me, still sobbing, by the arm and told me everything would be okay. A strange calmness overcame me. Watching, I saw the nurses cut the restraints from my wrist and ankles, remove the IVs, position my body, and cover me from head to toe. As the angels and I leave, the nurses were beginning to straighten up the ward in preparation for the morgue workers' arrival.

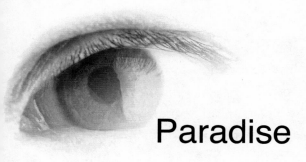

Paradise

The other angel had arrived, and it was time for us to leave. The angels took me by the arm and we were off, through the hospital wall into the cool night air. It was so refreshing. Confusing the feeling with something like being in a tunnel would be easy, only it wasn't a tunnel. It was like flying through space past white fluffy clouds. I could see light ahead. All around me was darkness and stars. One angel was flying ahead of me, and the other was at my side. The angel that was at my side told me to hold on to him and not turn loose, no matter what I saw or what happened. That was a little scary, and I asked, "Why, what's going to happen?"

Suddenly, there appeared strange and terrible looking creatures, a few at first, then more and more—some with the face like that of humans and some like strange flying animals or creatures I had never seen. They were the most horrible things I had ever seen. As they were trying to grab and take hold of me and were screaming for me to come and go with them, I actually felt them as they touched and grabbed at me. They told me I could have everything I would ever want if I would go and join with them. The angel holding on to me told me not to pay any attention to them explaining they were Lucifer's demons and angels that rebelled against God. The other angel was ahead of us fighting off the demons and fallen angels. I felt heat and smelled smoke as I looked around, and there I saw Lucifer, that old devil, laughing and shouting for the demons to bring me to him. I know it was Lucifer because that is what the angel called him. In the blink of an eye, surrounding us, there appeared flying Warrior angels, swordsmen on flying horses, angels with wings, and many other heavenly creatures that I had never seen before. They had all manner of weapons and used them to attack the demons and fallen angels. The battle was fierce, but the angels drove the demons away. The light was getting closer and closer, and then we were there, standing at the portal or entrance or gates of heaven.

At first, it seemed like we were in a fog or in a cloud. The fog began to thin, and I saw bright lights gleaming from behind a wall of white that looked like the keys on my dad's piano. One angel departed to my right and met with another angel. While they were talking, I looked back, and there was someone standing in front me. This person looked a lot like my eldest brother, Clyde, and somewhat like my sister, Earlene, but it couldn't be either of them; they were both alive and on earth.

"Who is this?" I asked the angel.

The angel explains to me that the staff of my blood (ancestors) selected my brother to meet me because they thought he would be the person I would most likely recognize. Seeing the familiarity in his face and that he favored my brother and sister would be less frightening to me.

"What is your name?" I asked.

"My name is Ralph; I am your brother."

"I don't have a brother named Ralph," I said.

The angel interrupted, saying that I never knew him because he died before I was born. I asked Ralph what happened to him. He told me how difficult it was for him to breathe after the accident. He said that Mom and Dad did everything they could, but he just couldn't keep breathing and died.

"I lived only a few months," he said.

The angel told me his body was buried at the old Presbyterian cemetery near where he was born. It was where Mom and Dad went to church when they first moved to Walden's Ridge.

Then I looked to his left and saw a boy and a girl dressed in white robes.

"Who are they?" I asked.

Ralph responded by saying they too were my brother and sister. They were the first set of twins born to our Mom and Dad. Curiously, I asked them why they were the only ones dressed in white robes. They told me it was because they died shortly after being born, and Mom and Dad didn't have time to name them.

"We are called the no-name twins," they told me. "We wait to be named by Mom or Dad when they arrive."

I asked the twins when and where they were born, how they died, and where were they buried.

While the twins were talking, I looked around at the crowd that had gathered. I saw no old people and no young children, infants, or babies, nor animals.

I interrupted the twins to ask the angel why there were no children or old people in paradise. He told me that all infants, children, old people, and those who die before birth, take on their heavenly bodies when they arrive, just as I had; that was why I was fully grown.

I turned back to the twins. My sister told me they died at childbirth, before I was born, and their bodies were buried near the window of Mom and Dad's bedroom on the mountain. I then asked Ralph and the twins if they knew why Mom and Dad never told any of us about them. They responded, "The pain of having their babies die before them has been so difficult to bear that they only talk about us between themselves. They blame each other for our death, which is why they fight so much."

As I continued to look around, I saw my grandmother, great-grandmother and great-grandfather. My grandmother died two years before I was born, and I had never seen a picture of her, but I knew who she was the moment I saw her. By now there were many people gathering about, maybe a few hundred or so. Some I recognized, but most I didn't. Some were dressed in suits and nice dresses spanning many generations, and some were dressed in clothing that appeared to be what they were wearing when they died. Standing in the crowd were two people who stood out as very different. One man was dressed like a knight in armor, holding his sword in his left hand with its tip touching the ground, his helmet being clutched with his right arm and his shield with his right hand and had what looked to me like a large flour sack pulled over his armor with a red cross across his chest. Not too far from him was another man dressed in a white robe wearing what looked to me like a pointed white hat (and, no, it wasn't a KKK hat). At that time, I had never seen anyone dressed like that, but as the years passed, I would learn that the man in the white robe with the pointed hat was

Carthusian Monk Maurice Chauncy who died in 1581 and the man in the Knight's regalia turned out to be a Templar Mason ancestor who took part in the crusades.

Those who had gathered in front of me began to take on a look of sadness.

"What's wrong?" I asked the angel. "They all look so sad now; what's happening? Isn't paradise a happy place?"

"It is a happy place, but they have learned that you need to go back and that has made them very sad," the angel responded.

"I don't want to go back," I said.

I continued to look around; asking if this was all there was to paradise. Just as I asked the question, the angel that had left earlier returned and whispered something to the angel standing next to me.

The angel then turned to me and said, "Yes, this is paradise, and there is much more—more than you can see, but we must wait here for a little while."

Being the pushy kid I was, I said to the angel that I wanted to see Jesus. The angel responded that I must wait a little longer. I wasn't having any of that and shouted, "I want to see Jesus!"

The angel calmed me by saying that even though I couldn't go in just yet, I would get to see Jesus. Just then, off to my right, I saw an angel dressed in regal attire coming from the portal of paradise and motioning for the second angel to come over to him.

"What is going on," I asked.

The first angel replied that the other angel was Gabriel, the archangel. After Gabriel had finished talking to the second angel, he came back and told us that Jesus had asked me to go back to earth.

"Back where?" I asked.

"To your body," the angel told me. "To your family, back to earth."

Well I didn't like that a bit and forcefully said, "No! I won't go."

Jesus sent Gabriel to have the angel ask me if I would return to earth and be there when he needed me for the future of my family. Jesus said that my death was more than Mom and Dad could bear and that the family wouldn't survive as a family unless I went back. I argued that I wanted to see Jesus and that I wouldn't go back until I did. The angels explained to me that once I passed through the portal of paradise, my body transformation would be complete and then I could never return to my earthly body.

"You cannot return to your body until the day the sons of man are resurrected if you don't go back now," the angel continued.

Still I refused to agree to return to earth without seeing Jesus.

It was then that the second angel again left and went to meet with Gabriel, the archangel. After their discussion, the archangel went back through the portal of paradise. Moments later, he returned and again spoke with the second angel.

After talking with Gabriel, the angel told me that Jesus promised to take care of me all the days of my life if I would return to earth. In addition, Jesus would give me eighty years and allow me to see things yet to come. Jesus said he wouldn't force me to return but asked that I agree to go. The angels were instructed to face me toward earth so I could see a vision of what would happen to my family if I didn't return to earth. What I saw was very disturbing.

As I turned toward earth, I had the feeling I was at the edge of heaven or a mountain looking out over the universe or a valley. It was like a camera zooming in on earth from the moon to the house where I had lived.

I looked toward my house to see a sheriff's patrol car and an unmarked car parked near the front steps of our house. Dad was being led down the steps by two deputy sheriffs. My dad's hands were behind his back in handcuffs. The deputies placed him in the backseat of the patrol car and drove off. As soon as Dad was put into the car, I saw my brothers and sister being led down the steps by a man and a woman placing them in the other car. I overheard them say they were going to the Bonny Oaks Orphans Home. Nowhere to be seen was my mom. When I asked the angel about my mom, the angel told me that my mother had died and that Dad was being blamed.

When I saw my dad in a jail cell, my heart broke because I adored my mom and dad and was devoted to them. The angel told me that I could prevent what I had seen by going back to earth. I didn't understand how I could prevent that from happening so I asked the angel. He said that would be made clear to me at the appropriate time.

Seeing that I was so distraught, the angels began showing me what was to come in the future and what was to happen to earth as this generation of man came to an end. Then I saw a beautiful woman and child standing in front of me. The woman looked very young, not more than a teenager. She was trim in her physical appearance and wearing a below-the-knees black dress. The child appeared to be about two or three years old with a bright and alert face that resembled the woman standing next to her. They were holding hands.

Puzzled, I asked, "Who are they?"

The angel told me that this woman was to be my wife and the little girl was to be my daughter. I don't recall ever having thought of having a wife or having any children. At the age of seven, that was so far from what was interesting to me that the image of the woman and child came as a startling surprise. The woman and child moved away from me, and their image faded away. I felt heat, smelled smoke, and heard all kinds of frightening noises.

"What is that?" I asked.

The angel turned me, and we walked toward what appeared to be the edge of heaven where I had a full view of earth. What I was seeing was what was to come as the end of this generation of man neared on earth. What I saw was so frightening that I haven't been able to put it out of my mind for more than six decades; I think about it every day. Wars, fires, earthquakes, conflicts, and death were occurring all around the world, and then it was upon the shores of America.

As the wars and conflicts unfolded, I saw in the north—what appeared to be in the direction of today's Russia—a great army moving south across Syria, all of Asia, and Africa. There was a portion of land bypassed by the conquerors. Now that I am old and understand some of earth's geography, I recognize that small portion of land to be Israel. All of the conquered joined with the army from the north to form the world's greatest military force. Having observed the conduct of politicians and governments for more than six decades, one would think someone would have been on alert against such coming together of countries.

The great army moved from the Asian continent and invaded all of Europe. Although the battles were fierce throughout most of Europe, it wasn't until they invaded England that the fighting became brutal. England put up such resistance that when the battle was lost, all of England lay in ruins. I recall as a little boy hearing a speech by Winston Churchill that went something like this: "We will fight them in air and on the sea, in the streets and in the alleys. We will never give up." Surely England had not lost that fighting spirit.

America was their next target. The invading force began its attack on the eastern coast of America. First were the rockets and bombs followed quickly by troops landing from the sea and from the air. New York, Philadelphia, Atlanta, Cincinnati, Chicago, Jacksonville all fell quickly. Turning toward the southwest of America, an invading force launched its attack on Southern California, Arizona, and New Mexico. The invading army didn't come from the sea or from the air; it came from South America across America's southern border. It wasn't long after the southern invasion that nuclear weapons began to fall all over America and Canada. It seemed no one was spared. America's ability to resist was very weak, and its ability to defend itself was in grave jeopardy.

Looking more closely I focused on the western coast of America where I saw great earthquakes and tremendous explosions intermixed with the invasions. Mountains rose, land disappeared, and crevices opened up across the land. A large portion of the West Coast of America slipped into the Pacific Ocean, creating a vast body of water between it and the mainland, becoming an island. Thousands attempted to swim to the mainland, only to drown in the ocean. So violent had the changes been that all ships and means of getting from the island to the mainland had been destroyed. Soon the food and water on the island disappeared. People were dying from starvation and dehydration, and many others were killed as they tried to take from each other. Cannibalism seemed to engulf the entire island. But soon, that same desperation would appear on the mainland of America and throughout the world.

Turning from the western coast, I looked toward the east coast and the Atlantic Ocean. Large cities lay in ruin as smaller cities came under attack and quickly fell to the invading forces. With America lying in ruins, conquerors from the east and south joined and began to assemble somewhere in Asia. Israel and remnants of resisting armies also began to assemble. During this time of strife, it didn't rain at all, anywhere on earth. All around, people and animals were afflicted by the most horrible diseases and sores. Dead bodies were lying everywhere, rotting and being eaten by fowl and beast. So much blood spilled from the dead bodies that rivers, lakes, and land turned pink. The earth became barren with only remnants of plant, human, and animal life remaining. All but about one-third of the earth had burned, and more than two-thirds of all its inhabitants had died.

The last battle was about to begin. All the forces of the world had assembled to destroy Israel. As the battle began, the great armies of the world came under attack from what looked like millions of angel warriors. When the great battle was over; the entire world army lay dead upon the ground. After more than twenty years of war, the heat, the noise of war, death, and destruction began to fade, and life began returning to earth. The landscape had the appearance of a carpet woven from dead bodies. Following the great conquering army's defeat the rain began to fall. Green plants started poking their heads up from the ground. The air became cleaner, and vegetation became thicker. As the earth renewed itself, I saw a bright glow coming from the east.

Slowly I turned and looked. As if looking from a tall mountain and beyond the eastern coast of America, a huge city was slowly descending toward earth from space, glowing as if it was illuminated by a grand light, covering what appeared to be all of the Asian and maybe the African continents. It looked very similar to the paradise where I was standing. Angels were everywhere, going back and forth from the city across the whole of the earth. There, in the midst of the city, Jesus Christ was awarding many of his followers with assignments and principalities of earth to govern. Lucifer, that old Satan, was bound and imprisoned, and peace covered the earth. Those souls that had been redeemed and whose names were written in a great book occupied the new city. How long did the wars and devastation last? The impression given to me was that the wars lasted for more than twenty years.

My attention was drawn back toward the rest of the earth where animals and people began to appear from places where they hid during the terrible time of destruction. Sadly, only a few remnants of humanity remained. As the rain fell and the animals began to emerge from their hiding places, I looked toward what was left of the

North and South American continents. As new plants, animal life, and remnants of humanity appeared, among it all laid the remnants of war—weapons, tanks, planes, missiles, machinery—and fallen manmade structures lay everywhere, rusting and decaying. At the time I didn't recognize the tanks, missiles, jet planes, and some of the other weapons of war. As a little boy, I had only seen the WWII planes as they flew overhead past our house on the mountain. But now I recognize those implements of war as being the implements of war now in use throughout the world.

A man and woman came out of their hiding place, a cave I think, holding hands and dressed in torn and tattered garments as they looked around and began to search for food and for seeds to plant in a garden. Others followed them, as all around the earth life was being restored. Continents were reshaped, and in the great land of North America, an enormous lake was formed in the upper-middle portion of America.

Mountains had fallen; canyons disappeared; the courses of rivers were changed, and much land disappeared. Almost all of Florida disappeared along with much of the east coast. In the west, the greatest reshaping took place from the upper portion of Mexico to Oregon. Portions of Texas and Arizona were now lakes. What had been the deserts of the west were now green and lush with trees and vegetation. Asia, Africa, Europe, and the world over became lush with vegetation, clear water, lakes, and rivers, and an abundance of fish, fowl, and animal life.

As I watched the new earth develop, the angels interrupted and turned me back toward the gates of paradise. At last, I saw Jesus emerging from a building dressed in a white robe and walking toward the steps to greet the men who had gathered. Imagine my surprise when he didn't look like any of the pictures I had seen in Sunday school or anywhere else. However, since that time and as I have grown older, I have seen pictures that are remarkably similar to his likeness. It isn't something that I can prove, but my conviction is that somewhere in time, one or more very talented artists have experienced what I experienced and recorded it on canvas. A few years ago while watching a program on the History channel, I saw a painting that accurately captured the image of the demons that I saw on my way to paradise. Surely, no one could conjure those exact images from their imagination; I just don't think it possible. One thing has been made perfectly clear to me. Humanity can cause a delay or shifts within periods of time, but humanity cannot prevent them unless all humanity totally rejects evil.

There were ten or twelve men gathered around the steps as I heard Jesus Christ call some of them by name. They were referred to as the elders, and among them were Adam, Moses, Esau, and Abraham. Strange voices came from underneath the throne that sat at the head of the steps, asking something like how much longer must they wait for vengeance. As the men talked with Jesus, I saw in front of them, across the river of life, millions of people; it was impossible to count them. Even now there isn't any way I could estimate how many I saw. Approaching the portal of paradise, I could see the wonders of paradise. The tree of knowledge, the river of life, mansions, streets that looked like glistening metal, foundations and buildings made of colorful and transparent stones, walls that have the appearance of pearl, and so much more. As people would walk past where Jesus Christ and the men were, I could hear them singing and saying, "Worthy is the Lamb of God."

As I watched, Jesus Christ turned and looked at me and smiled as he motioned for the angel Gabriel to come near him. They spoke for a moment and then Gabriel came to me with a message from Jesus. Then it was time to go.

The Miracle Boy Returns Home

The trip back to earth was about the same as it was going, except there wasn't any bright light at the end, and we didn't encounter any demons or Lucifer. The trip was quick, and we soon reached the hospital room. The room was dark, except for the light shining through the Venetian Blinds in the hall windows. I stared at my body covered from head to foot with a sheet. For a moment, the angels and I just stood there in silence. The angels had a sad look on their face. I was beginning to feel all alone. This was my last chance to change my mind and return to paradise. Although I loved my parents very much, my future life on earth could in no way compare to paradise.

It was with sadness that I asked the angels how to get back into my body. The angels too were sad, with tears in their eyes they pulled the sheet from the face of my body.

"So how do I get back in there?" I asked again.

At first, I thought they were joking when they told me to jump into my mouth when they opened it.

"Jump like you are jumping into a swimming pool—feet first, and we will do the rest," they told me.

I looked at them like they were crazy, but when I saw the seriousness in their faces, I knew I should do as they instructed. Jumping feet first into my mouth felt like I was being sucked down into my body. The sensation I had was of being cold, and I was frightened. Almost instantly I could see through my body's eyes so I knew I was back in my body. It was strange at first. I could only move my eyes, talk, and hear. I told the angels that it was cold in here.

"In a moment, it will begin to get warm," they said. The angels told me to relax and go to sleep, that they were going to pull the sheet over my head, and when I awakened, everything would be fine.

Early in the morning while it was still dark, looking through the fabric of the sheet, I saw the image of a woman come into the ward and move toward me. She didn't turn on the lights, but I could see her through the sheet because the glow from the corridor lights partially illuminated the room. I couldn't take my eyes off of her as she came up to my bed and pulled the sheet from my face. She was the most beautiful woman I had ever seen. My eyes must have been as big as saucers. There was something about this woman that was breathtaking. It was as though I had known her all my life and had just been reunited. Her skin was glowing with a hue that can only be described as a burnt golden color. Her hair was black as coal. Her voice was soothing and musical. She told me to not be afraid. When I asked her who she was, she said her name was Mary.

"Mary?"

"Yes, my son sent me; I am here to take care of you and the children. Do you know where you are?" she asked.

I told her that I thought I was in a hospital. She asked if I knew which hospital.

"No."

"You are in the Children's Hospital." (In the ensuing years I would learn the children's hospital was the T.C. Thompson Children's Hospital in Chattanooga, Tennessee.)

She then asked me what I remembered. I told her I remembered getting sick, hallucinating, and going to paradise.

"Do you remember anything else?" she asked.

I couldn't remember anything else.

She gently rubbed my face and ran her fingers through my hair as she explained that all of the disease had been removed from my body.

She continued, "Because of the high fever, you may not remember many things. It may be difficult, but we will always be here to help you through those times."

As she pulled the sheet back over my face, she said, "Sleep; they will be here soon."

They, of course, were the housekeepers.

Lights in the hospital corridor were dim, and there was only an occasional sound as the children slept so peacefully. It was unusually quiet that morning as a deputy sheriff stood outside the quarantined ward. Inside the darkened ward lay a single seven-year-old body awaiting collection for cremation by order of the County Health Authority as a precaution to prevent the spreading of a very contagious disease. Outside, the moon and stars were shining brightly with only a few puffy clouds floating overhead from time to time. We dreamt of nights like these where we could lie on our back and gaze into the heavens and dream of wonders to behold.

Just before the breaking of dawn, two house-keepers dressed in protective clothing arrived to sanitize the quarantined ward. The six-bed ward was empty, except for one white metal bedside table, one hospital bed with rail sides, and two IV poles, not connected to the body but seeming to stand watch. The housekeepers were surprised to find the body still in the room. The morgue workers should have already collected the body for cremation.

One of the housekeepers said to the other that she wanted to get a look at the little boy that had died during the night.

"Do you want to look?" asked the housekeeper.

"No, I don't like to look at dead bodies. Not even at a funeral," the other housekeeper responded.

Alone, the housekeeper walked slowly to the side of the lone bed. She reached out her hand slowly to lift the sheet from my face.

As she did, I gave her a big smile and said, "Hi!" Whoowee, you should have seen her. She jumped as if she had seen a ghost. She screamed and ran from the ward toward the nurses' station, screaming, "He's alive! He's alive!"

The other housekeeper was so scared that she just stood frozen with her hands to her face staring in shock as she stood, speechless.

Nurses scrambled to put on protective gowns and mask as they ran toward my ward. A couple of nurses didn't take time to put on their protective clothing and burst into the ward. When the head nurse arrived a moment later, she ordered everyone without protective clothing to leave the room immediately and to disinfect to prevent the spreading of the disease to the rest of the patients on the floor. It had been more than two hours since I died. The nurses were frantically trying to contact the doctor who had left the hospital after declaring my time of death. The doctor was stunned when they awoke him at home. He couldn't believe what he was hearing. He immediately jumped out of the bed and called Mom and Dad. As quickly as possible, he made his way down the mountain to the hospital.

Mom and Dad had remained at the hospital until I was declared dead. It took all their strength to leave me at the hospital knowing they had seen me for the last time. After all, they had already buried three children, and I was number four. It seemed more than they could bear. My death could easily split the family apart.

As with most parents, when children die, they blame each other or someone else. Most folks just cannot accept that sometimes bad things just happen. Mom and Dad had been blaming each other for the deaths of the first three children for years. That was probably the basis of all their arguments and fights. It looked like it could only get worse.

When they arrived home, they woke my siblings and gathered them in the living room. After they had explained what had happened to me, they formed a prayer circle on the living room floor. Each of my siblings, except for my youngest brother, who at the time was only three years old, kneeled and formed a prayer circle. They each began to pray for God to restore my life. The family had been praying, what seemed for hours, when the telephone rang. Reluctantly Dad broke from the prayer circle and answered the phone to hear the doctor's excitement as he told Dad I was alive. As soon as they heard the news, the family jumped with joy, and Mom fell back to her knees, praying and thanking God for restoring me to life. Dad knelt down with her, holding her as they both cried with joy. They collected themselves, and the entire family began to dress to go to the hospital.

They were almost ready to leave for the hospital when Dad heard a noise at the front of the house and saw someone affix a sign to the front door. When he opened the front door, the person who had affixed the sign had reached the gate at the road. Dad looked at the sign and saw the house and property had been placed on quarantine. Similar signs were being placed around the perimeter of the entire property. In addition, a sheriff's patrol car was parked at the front gate and driveway entrances. No one would be allowed to leave or come onto the property for the next fifteen days. Food would be delivered by the health department and left at the front gate for the family. The Hamilton County Health Department said the quarantine was necessary because the meningitis I had was so contagious someone else in the family may have become infected and could spread the disease. For the entire quarantine time, a deputy and/or someone from the County Health Department stood guard at the property, ensuring no one left the quarantined area. The County Health Department delivered food products to the house on a regular basis. Sadly, Dad had to tell the family about the quarantine.

Dad was convinced that the meningitis came from our cow's fresh milk and that she would have to be destroyed. The next day Dad took his rifle, killed old Betsy and buried her at the far end of our property. For the next two weeks my family would wait out the quarantine cautiously watching each other for any signs of the disease.

The on-call doctor arrived in short order. I was happy and smiling, trying to tell the doctor and nurses I was fine and not sick anymore that Jesus had cured me. They didn't pay any attention to me and immediately began to administer medication and sticking IVs back into my hands and arms. I was so excited about what had happened to me while I was dead that I couldn't stop talking about it. They started calling me Miracle Boy. When things settled down, the nurses gave me a sponge bath, brought me clean pajamas and tried to get me to eat some Jell-O, but I said no. I wanted ice cream. They found me a Popsicle and generally made over me like I was something very special.

While the doctors were working on me after they found me alive, it didn't take long for it to sink in that no one believed what I had said about going to paradise.

After being found alive by the housekeepers and all the fuss that was made by the hospital staff, not much else happened throughout the week-end until Monday morning. Friday, Saturday, and Sunday passed with only the doctors and nurses constantly coming into the ward doing stuff to me. I had so many shots that my arms, legs and buttocks looked like pincushions. One nurse even cried when it came time for her to give me more shots because she said she couldn't find a spot that hadn't been used. Even now when given a CT scan at the Mayo Clinic as a follow-up precaution to my cancers and heart attacks, the Radiologist's notes reflect the excessive amount of scar tissue found in my body from needle pricks.

Still in quarantine, and high fever having taken most of my memory, I wasn't expecting anyone other than the hospital staff to come see me. However, on Monday, a preacher came to see me. When he entered the room, I thought I recognized him, but I didn't. He came over to my bed and introduced himself as Lee Roberson, pastor of the Highland Park Baptist Church.

"Monday is my day to do hospital rounds; I have been to Erlanger and Memorial hospitals to visit with church members, and when I looked at my cards to see if any of our church member's children were admitted to this hospital, I didn't see any, so I drove on by. As I drove a little past the hospital, I had the feeling that I should go back. Thinking maybe it was the Holy Spirit talking to me, I turned around. The admissions office told me they didn't know of any of my church member's children being here; however, they said I might want to see their Miracle Boy."

Intrigued by their description of what had happened to me he agreed to visit with me.

It turned out that the preacher was the same preacher who had introduced me to Jesus Christ in the tent revival. However, at that first meeting he did not recognize me either. Thinking we may have met he had his secretary check his church's records for my name, and there it was with the dates of my accepting Jesus at the tent revival. He talked with me about my experience in paradise and said this is the first time he had met anyone that related such an experience. During our talk he related to me that he and his wife had recently lost their daughter Joy. After our talk he prayed with me and gave me a toy. Each Monday I was in the hospital, he would come and visit with me, and each time he would give me a toy. One toy had several flat pieces of painted wood held together by long ribbons. When the toy was tilted to one side then the other, the blocks of wood would cascade down the ribbon. Another toy was a stick about six inches long with a wooden ball attached with a string and you had to try to catch the wood ball in a little cup at the end of the stick. Another was a coloring book and crayons.

That same Monday Dr. Hair, the doctor that was at my bedside when I died, brought a team of doctors into the room to examine me. They talked with me, asking many questions, examining me physically, and then left the room. After the visit, Dr. Hair called my parents with the sad news that I had lost most of my memory. He thought it best not to tell them that I didn't even remember them.

For about a week, the nurses would come in and massage and exercise my legs. Up until then, I hadn't been allowed to get out of the bed. This day the nurses came into the room and said it was time for me to get up and walk. They said that if I didn't start to exercise by walking that my muscles would deteriorate and that it would make recovery very difficult. They lowered the bed rail and helped me sit upright on the side of the bed telling me to slowly let myself down and put my feet on the floor and stand. When I did I fell to the floor, unable to hold up my weight. I couldn't make my legs move. The nurses picked me up and put me into bed, raised the rail, and left the room, telling me not to worry, that it happens sometimes and that everything would be all right.

It wasn't long before several doctors and nurses came into the room and began examining me by touching, pulling, and pricking me with pins. I couldn't feel the pins prick my legs or feet and couldn't move my toes. It seems that I was paralyzed from the waist down.

Late that night when the corridor lights were dimmed, Mary awakened me. She was the same Mary that I saw when I first awoke from returning to my body. I was excited to see her because I had only seen her once. She said, "Be quiet," and then began to undress me and turned me over on my stomach. Then she took her hands and beginning at the base of my skull slowly moved her hands down my spine, continuing down one leg and the other hand down the other leg. She did that several times, and when she was through, my feet and legs began to tingle like someone was sticking them with a million pins. She then dressed me and told me to go back to sleep, that when I awoke everything would be okay and that I would be able to walk.

The next morning when the nurses came around to care for me, I told them I wanted to try to walk. They told me no, that the doctors would see me later in the day. When the doctors arrived to examine me, I told them I could move my legs and toes. One doctor took a pin and began to prick my skin at different places on my body, legs and feet. I could feel all the pinpricks. They couldn't understand what happened. When I tried to explain what had happened, they just humored me. Finally, they agreed to let me try to walk and instructed the nurses to help me stand beside the bed. When they did, I was able to stand and started to take a step, but they stopped me. The doctors order therapy on my legs. Later that day the nurses let me walk with them across the room and back.

Early the next day, a team of doctors and nurses came into the room and sat me up in the bed. They put my head between my legs. One nurse got up into the bed with me and held my head very still between my legs. After they had me in a position where I couldn't move, I felt a needle go into my back and into my spine. It really hurt, but I couldn't cry out because of the way they were holding me. After it was over, I was told they had given me a spinal tap by inserting a needle into my spine draining some fluid.

One afternoon two nurses rolled a baby bed into my ward. The baby couldn't have been more than one or two months old. When I asked the nurses why they were bringing the baby into my room, they told me the baby had an open spine and meningitis. There wasn't much of a chance that she would survive, but if she did, it would be very difficult for her and her parents. The parents would have to take care of her every hour of every day because the baby would be like a vegetable, and care would be expensive. Over the next few days, I watched the baby very carefully. She didn't move very much, and she didn't cry much either. Nurses would come in from time to time, give her a baby bottle, and change her diaper.

On one occasion watching the baby, I felt ill. She had filled her diaper and was taking her finger and eating the contents. A nurse came in to see about the baby, so I asked about what the baby had done, and the nurse said it didn't really matter and that the baby would die shortly anyway.

A strange thing occurred on the day the baby died. I was lying in my bed, mostly staring at the ceiling, when I heard this faint noise coming from the baby. At that moment the door to my ward opened and in walked Mary. She glanced at me as she walked toward the baby and said, "I've come for the baby."

She reached over the crib to the baby, turned the baby on its back, touching the baby with her hands, and as she touched the baby, I had a sense that something left the baby and went into Mary's arms. At that moment, Mary folded her arms up over her chest as though she was clutching something and walked toward the door. She held her left arm and hand up, covering her chest as she used her right hand to open the door and exit the room.

Within a few minutes nurses came in, wrapped the baby in sheets and took her away. Even though the image of that baby has haunted me my entire life, I am so glad I was there with her so she didn't have to die alone.

I had been in the hospital two weeks when a nurse came into the room and told me that the quarantine had been lifted on my family and they wanted to see me. She asked if I wanted to see them.

"Yes," I said. "I would like to see them."

I was so excited. She told me they couldn't come into the hospital room because the ward was still under quarantine, but they were standing out front of the hospital on the steps with my brothers and sister. The nurse rolled my bed to the window, and I looked out for my parents and family. There were people standing around on the front steps of the hospital, but I couldn't find anyone I recognized. I asked the nurse what had happened to them. She came over to the window and pointed them out to me. I didn't recognize any of them. Even though I was happy to see people who were supposed to be my family, for the rest of the day I felt alone and empty. The nurses were great, but that didn't make the time go by any faster for me. Since I didn't remember my family nor did I remember my home, the hospital room became my home, and I no longer wanted to go anywhere.

Time had come for me to go home. My parents had been waiting down by the front door because, even though I was well, the room where I stayed was still under quarantine. I couldn't understand why there were so many nurses gathered around me as they took me in a wheelchair to the front of the hospital. When I asked why, they told me a big crowd was waiting for the Miracle Boy to leave the hospital.

"Why?" I asked.

"Don't you know?" the nurse asked.

"No."

"Well, you are quite a celebrity. There are newspaper reporters and photographers out there waiting for you."

I didn't know what reporters and photographers were, so I became a little apprehensive. I was beginning to maybe look forward to leaving the hospital and going home, even though it was very scary. I was now aware that I had no memory of my brothers or sisters, and that was frightening. I couldn't even remember their names. The nurses and hospital workers answered the reporter's questions except one. And when asked, I told them I felt fine. My parents greeted me with smiles, hugs, and laughter. Many of the nurses and hospital workers who had tended me came to see me off and cheered as their Miracle Boy departed.

Going home was difficult. On the way home, my parents told me that they didn't bring my brothers or sister because they didn't want them to know I had lost my memory. Being next to the youngest child, they thought my brothers might taunt me if they knew I couldn't remember anything. They took their time driving home, and on the way, Mom had me memorize the names of my siblings. I tried as best I could to remember the names, but it was almost impossible. To remember five new names, in addition to my own name and parents' names was just too much. My parents were great; they even gave me a Mickey Mouse watch as a welcome home gift because I was in the hospital during my eighth birthday. The watch puzzled me because I didn't know what it was or how to use it. Mom reminded me that I learned how to tell time in the second grade. When I asked what the second grade was, she broke down in tears. My brothers and sister were never told that I had lost my memory, making it even more difficult growing up. For the next five decades, I felt that no one really understood me, except perhaps my sister. Even now, there remains a feeling of communications failure with whomever I am conversing with.

Arriving home, I was happy to see people who knew me, even if I didn't know them. After getting out of the car, my brothers and sister came out of the house to greet me. My parent's word was all I had that they were my siblings. It didn't take my sister long to figure out that I couldn't remember her. After some nagging I relented and told her that I could only remember a few basic things, like how to talk, walk, eat, and a few other things, but mostly I only remember being so ill and how painful it was and going to paradise. She assured me I shouldn't worry because she would teach me everything I had forgotten.

The Sunday after going home, when the family had finished breakfast, Sister was cleaning up the kitchen. The twins were helping her by cleaning up the table, and my eldest brother was in the living room. Dad was in the living room reading the newspaper. Mom had gone into her bedroom to make up the bed. Wanting to find out about Ralph and the unnamed twins I had met in paradise, I followed her into the bedroom.

The moment I mentioned them, Mom fell down to the floor, begging me not to hurt or punish her, that she was very sorry. Dad, hearing her scream, came rushing into the bedroom to see what was wrong. He thought I had done something to hurt her and was preparing to punish me when she stopped him. She told him I knew about the twins, and he began to hold Mom and comfort her until he was able sit her on the bed.

By now, the other children were sticking their heads through the door to see what was going on. Dad got up, closed the door to the bedroom, and told Mom they needed to tell me everything. After they told me about the twins, Dad asked me if I wanted to see where they were buried. I said yes, and Dad took me to the window and pointed to a small area of the yard and said that was their grave. Then I asked about Ralph, and they told me what had happened to him, how long he had lived, and where he was buried. Later they took me to the cemetery to see Ralph's grave.

Five decades later I told my two surviving brothers about the first set of twins, Ralph, and where they were buried. I was surprised to find out that they didn't know about them. After telling them where the first set of twins were buried they remembered the small section of yard outside the bedroom where Dad and Mom would never let us play. My brothers always wondered why we couldn't play there.

It was now into the winter season. It was cold, all the leaves had fallen, and there was frost on the ground. All of the children, except my younger brother, had walked to the small community center for Sunday school. Upon returning home, we immediately sensed the tension. Something was wrong, but we had learned long ago to avoid our parents when they were fussing with each other. Evidently, the tension had been brewing for some time because they were almost to the exploding point when the family sat down for dinner. Little did I know that in a few minutes, the moment for which I had returned to earth would be upon me.

We had sat down for Sunday dinner when Dad asked Mom to pass the salt. She looked at him, picked up the salt shaker, and threw it at him, and the fight was on. It escalated until they were becoming physically threatening to each other and chasing each other around the house. When Mom went into their bedroom and emerged with Dad's rifle, Dad ran out of the house to avoid Mom. Immediately Mom took off after him and they met at the front steps to the house. Somewhere along the way, Dad had picked up a madax.

The moment they confronted each other, time seemed to stand still. I was startled when I felt a hand on my shoulder. I could see all my brothers and sister; I looked around to see an angel with her hand on my shoulder. She said my time had come to fulfill my responsibility and that I had to act immediately.

"Act? Do what? Who are you?"

"I am Ruth, your guardian angel. Now get in there between them." I was going to argue with her that I couldn't do it when she pushed me in between them. In an instant, as I faced Dad, a look of terror came upon his face, and Mom stood motionless.

One angel grabbed the madax Dad was holding, stopping him from swinging, and another angel knocked the rifle out of Mom's hands. At that moment, I didn't know they saw the host of warrior angels surrounding them carrying weapons, swords, shields, and other instruments of battle. Mom and Dan fell to the ground on their knees. The angel that had taken me by the shoulder came to me and told me that everything would be all right from then on and for me to be at peace. My eldest brother ran to Dad to help him up and Sister ran to Mom. As they helped each other up, Mom and Dad took hold of each other. All the angels turned and departed into the heavens, and I felt calm and peaceful.

Later that afternoon Dad called me to the front porch where he and Mom were sitting in the swing. As they spoke to me, I could tell they were very shaken. I had never seen them afraid of anything before. They asked me if I saw the people on horseback and on foot that were carrying the swords and things. I said yes. I had seen them and was surprised that they had seen them too. They asked if I knew who they were. I told them that they were warrior angels sent to protect me. Dad asked what the angels would have done if either of them had tried to hurt me. I responded that the angels would have killed them or anyone that harmed me during the fight.

Mom and Dad were strong moral Christian people, even though they were often at odds with each other. They had a great fear of God and his power. What they had witnessed at the steps had really shaken them. From that time forth, my parents were very fearful of punishing me, for fear they would raise the wrath of God and the warrior angels would return to punish them.

In the years that followed, I wish I had realized how they felt and had known to tell them to treat me like the rest of the kids, but I didn't know. Dad only spanked me once after that day. Before he began punishing me, he asked me if the angels would seek vengeance. I assured him that what I had done deserved punishment and that nothing would happen to him.

As for Mom, she too was fearful of punishing me, and on the only occasion she started to punish me, I stopped her by simply telling her that I was old enough that just reminding me of my wrongs would be enough. She too became very fearful, crying as we hugged. I told her that I loved her very much and thanked her for being such a good mom.

Another thing had become very apparent to me. I needed to know right from wrong. Most of us learn right from wrong, or the basis of right from wrong, at a very early age, and I am sure I did also. By the time we are six years old, we should have pretty good grasp of what we should do and what we shouldn't do. When I lost my memory I also lost all right and wrong teachings. Over the next fifteen to twenty years, I made mistakes from not having that knowledge.

It never occurred to me, after I lost my memory, that when someone says they wish something would happen to make their life better, they didn't really mean it because they knew it was wrong or illegal. I just saw it as something that needed to happen so it would help them feel better so sometimes I would make it happen.

In church one Sunday when the collection plate was passed in front of me I decided it was okay for me to take some money out of the collection plate. After all, I reasoned, the purpose of taking up a collection was to get money to help those that didn't have any, and I didn't have any. Of course I should have known better and of course I was caught and severely chastised by the ushers taking up the collection and the elders of the church. It was only then I learned and realized that the collection plate wasn't for me but it was for the church. The church elders wasted no time in making my parents aware of what I had done. Still afraid to punish me, my parents gave me a good talking to and said if I was to grow up to be a real man I would have to make my misdeed up to the church. Over the years I have made it a point to make extra contributions to the church in the form of the tithes, offerings, and gifts to make amends for those actions. Additionally, I have confessed my misdeed to the church elders and I can only hope that Jesus Christ, as my atonement, has accepted my actions.

Neither did I realize that it was wrong to take a toy from a store or from someone if I didn't have a toy to play with. Again, I got away with it until my father caught me with a new toy. He knew that he hadn't bought it for me, and he had asked Mom if she had bought it for me, and he knew my brothers or sister would never buy me a toy, leaving only one assumption—I had stolen the toy. He inquired as to where I got the toy, and I had no problem telling him because I didn't know it was wrong. My father wasn't harsh or unkind about what I did but simply said, "You need to come with me."

He put me in the front seat of his truck, and we started down the road. As we traveled, he explained to me that taking a toy without paying for it was wrong and that I would be punished. We arrived at the store, went inside, and sought out the manager. He took me to the manager with the toy in hand. Following my father's instructions, I told the manager what I had done, and I apologized. I made no excuses because my father had told me that a man doesn't make excuses for his actions. A real man will always take responsibility for his actions and take whatever consequences follow. A few weeks later dad would take me to a section of town called Onion Bottom. At Onion Bottom was the county chain gang and workhouse. The workhouse was sometimes called poorhouse or debtor's prison. When we stopped at the entrance dad got out of his truck and went inside. A few minutes later he came and told me to get out of the truck and go inside with him. Inside he turned me over to the jailer, a big, tough-looking man. The jailer took me by the arm with strong grip and put me in one of the jail cells with some very scary men shackled together with chains. They didn't hurt me but they didn't cut me any slack either. When my father returned from what seemed like hours and hours I was an emotional wreck, scared to death. As we left the jailhouse he said to me, "Son, if you continue to do wrong this is where you will spend the rest of your life." That was a bitter lesson to learn, but one I really needed to learn. I really needed to relearn those lessons of right and wrong that my father had taught me at an earlier age. Only then, after we talked about right and wrong, did my dad understand that I had lost all the lessons he had taught me growing up.

Challenges
in School

When school started, I needed to know how to write my name, say my ABCs, and other basic things to get me through the first few days of school. That was the first time I had thought about school and wanted to know what it was like. My sister told me everything she could remember so that I would have some idea of what to expect. For the next two weeks, my sister and I spent almost every hour of every day together as she taught me everything I could take in. Mostly my grades would be just high enough to keep me at the bottom of the class.

I wasn't looking forward to the first day back to school. Mom warned me that it would be very trying and difficult for me. My sister took me to my third grade classroom and instructed me to find a desk and then left to go to her own class. Nathan L. Bachman Elementary School was a small country school with first grade through the eighth grade. Other children were coming into the classroom and speaking to me, calling me Wilburn, my middle name, but I couldn't remember any of them. I smiled and said hello. The teacher came into the classroom and told everyone to sit down. She asked each student to stand and state their name.

When it became my turn, I stood up and told everyone my name was James. That was my first name, and it was the name that sounded the best to me. The other kids in the classroom began laughing and pointing their finger at me saying, "That isn't your name. That isn't your name!"

I was briefly scolded by the teacher and told to use my middle name. She instructed me that I had always been called in school by my middle name and that was the name I was to use. I sat down, embarrassed and humiliated.

Later the teacher asked the students to come to the front of the classroom one at a time and tell what happened to them over the summer. When it came my turn to tell my story, I could only remember the illness and my visit to paradise. I had gotten to the part of my story where I was going to paradise, telling about the demons and the angels, when the class began to jeer and laugh. This angered the teacher, and she stopped me from completing my story. Forcefully, she told me to go into the hall and wait for her. I did as she asked.

After she had calmed the classroom, she came into the hall and grabbed me by the arm. Walking fast as she could, holding onto my arm, she took me to the principal's office. After telling the principle what I had said in the classroom, she turned and went back to her class. The principal told me it was my fault for causing the class to become unruly by making up such a ridiculous story, and as my punishment, he gave me several licks with a wooden paddle. On the paddle he had the words *Board of Education*.

That evening I told Mom and Dad about my treatment at school and how the principal treated and spanked me. That evening they paid a visit to the principal's home. I had to remain in the car with Mom while Dad went in and had a talk with the principal. Mom became worried when Dad didn't come out as soon as she thought he should. She told me to stay put in the car, and she went in to check on Dad. After a while, they came out, and from that day forward, I never had any problems with the principal.

It is hard to forget the terrible things that were said to me. From comments my classmates would make to me, it was evident that I had become a joke and a topic in their home. Some would call me names, tell me I was a liar about what happened to me, and even accused of faking my illness. Some of those self-righteous better-than-thou older people even called me a devil, or worse, they called me an antichrist because of the things I spoke about. They said no one but a devil would know such things. I have never researched what was printed in the newspapers about "Miracle Boy," but whatever it was, it caused my parents to never subscribe to the newspaper thereafter.

It wasn't long before we moved from the mountain to the city; I didn't like the city at all. Starting into another grade at a new school was traumatic. There was an elementary school about one thousand yards from our house in the city, but the school board wouldn't let me go to school there. They said I wasn't a fit student to associate with the class of students there and the parents would raise a protest. Every morning for the next year I walked about a quarter of a mile to the bus stop and boarded a commercial bus that took me to a rural section of the county. That school was considered rather low on the education and social totem pole, so it shouldn't matter if I attended there. My parents fought with the school board until they were exhausted finally relinquishing when the school board said I could attend a school closer to our house the following year if I didn't cause any problems that year. I only made one friend at school that year. His father was a Presbyterian preacher who didn't like me at all after he connected me with the Miracle Boy stories in the paper. After playing at my friend's house one afternoon, he told his wife to make sure their son never played with me again, that I wasn't a fit playmate or friend for the son of a preacher. That really hurt because he was the only friend I had that year, even if it was only for a little while.

The next year I enrolled in the Missionary Ridge Elementary School near our home, a much better school. My teacher was Ms. Clear, and what a great woman she was. She understood how far behind the other students I was and pushed me relentlessly to catch up. She refused to accept the stories in the paper from a few years earlier and also helped me with getting along with other classmates. For all these decades, my memory won't let go of Ms. Clear.

Time had arrived for me to transfer to the seventh grade at the junior high school my brothers attended. Their objections and my bad grades, caused by my loss of memory, became a big problem. My brothers put up such a fuss that I wasn't allowed to enroll in school at their local junior high school. I think they were ashamed of me. As twins, they always had each other as companions, and I understood, but it still hurt that I couldn't be a companion with them. Mom told me that it has always been that two is company and three is a crowd.

There was only one other school available where the school board would let me attend the seventh grade and that was at Chattanooga Central High School where they were experimenting with integrating the seventh and eighth grades with the ninth through the twelfth grade high school classes. I wasn't at all happy with the arrangement, but because my sister was a senior that year, it was okay, and she promised to look after me. However, the principal and vice principal of the high school had other ideas. They convinced the county school board that I was retarded because my grades were so bad. They also accused me of cheating on an IQ exam. When my parents were notified that I was going to be transferred to a local vocational trade school, they demanded a meeting.

The meeting took place at the high school with all parties attending. As I listened, I overheard the principal tell my parents that I would never be able to support myself, let alone a family. With my mental ability, I would be lucky to hold a job sweeping streets or working as an unskilled laborer on a construction crew. Additionally, they insisted I should be made sterile so I couldn't reproduce, because there was no way I could ever support a family. They were convinced I was destined to become a welfare burden to the county. My parents came out fighting. They knew what had happened to my memory and were convinced that I wasn't retarded. The school principals were mistaking my loss of memory with mental illness. My parents wouldn't even consider the school administrators' point of view and refused to permit me to be transferred or sterilized.

All this came about just after the school administered an IQ test to all seventh and eighth graders entering the high school. The school principal and vice principal accused me of cheating based on my school record. They had no idea that only a few years earlier I had lost all my memory of things I had learned in school. When the cheating accusation was brought to my parent's attention at the meeting, my parents demand to know why they thought I cheated on the IQ test.

The school administrators (educated elite) said no one with school grades as bad as mine could do as well as I did on the IQ test. They didn't know how, but they just knew I had cheated. Dad demanded proof, and when they couldn't provide proof, they agreed to a compromise. I would have to take a different IQ test and how I did on the test would determine my school fate.

I was taken into a classroom with my parents and school administrators, and over my parents' objections, they had me remove all my clothing except my under shorts. They examined me for any writing or notes or whatever written on my body. It was as though they suspected I somehow knew I would have to take another IQ exam and wrote all kinds of answers on my body. Sometimes the stupidity of the educated elite scares the hell out of me. Afterward, only the test giver and I remained in the room. She immediately scored the test and the school administration couldn't believe what they saw. I had scored one point below the original IQ test score, forcing the school administration to abandon their demands of transferring me to the vocational trade school. (In retrospect, I probably would have enjoyed the vocational school because I love building and making things with my hands). Next year I would be allowed to go to Brainerd Junior High School after my brothers graduated.

One never gets used to that kind of treatment. It had occurred off and on ever since I came back to earth. If I had known what an IQ test was and what it meant, maybe I wouldn't have felt so low. What the school administrators had said about me echoed in my head for years. Being convinced by them that I was retarded, and I interpreted that as being ignorant, reinforced in me the idea that school was a waste of time and all I needed to do was only what I had to do to graduate and get a diploma. Someone had told me that as long as I had a diploma, it would put me equal to all the other kids and that no one would actually go back to see how bad my school grades were.

When looking at the transcript of my junior and senior high school grades, it is easy to see the difficulty that I had in absorbing the material and obtaining passing grades. My attitude toward school didn't help with my grades either. It was in Junior ROTC I found the best outlet for my energies. I took that training very seriously and enjoyed it very much.

My year in the seventh grade would become one of several pivotal years of my life. It was during the seventh grade that I left my paper route and took a job working at a Kroger grocery store across the street from my school. John Reece was the store manager that I had met as my Sunday school teacher at the Highland Park Baptist Church. After meeting him, I asked if there was any part-time work at his store, and he said yes. However, it wasn't until I went to work at the store that I really felt this man's influence on my life. Other than my dad, if there is one man in my more than seven decades of living, John would be the person that had the greatest positive influence on me as a person. I remember John was the first person to look at me as a regular person, nothing special, with nothing wrong with me. He treated me as though I was someone important and that began to raise my feeling of self-worth. I didn't feel retarded around him. True, I did still feel ignorant because there were so many things I didn't know, but John never treated me like I was ignorant. He taught me many things about working, diligence, and integrity, Christian living, and just how to be a normal moral person. My employment with Kroger and John Reece lasted until after I had finished high school. I left Kroger for the United States Air Force, and when I returned from military service, the first person, other than my parents and girlfriend, I wanted to see was John. He was very gracious to me and made a place for me to work at his new store. He became a very special pivotal influencing factor in my life. Having known John began a turnaround toward a maturity that I suppose most young boys find much earlier in life. I very much regret that I put much of what he taught me aside during my military service and ensuing years. However, by putting many of those teachings aside, I obtained knowledge of how other people lived that I never could have obtained otherwise. That knowledge helped me economically enormously in the years to come but spiritually it did great damage.

Another pivotal point was a realization that I was somewhat different and that my approach about many things wasn't conventional. At church when I would speak of things, without saying that I had been in paradise, those comments usually were met with skepticism. It was from the skepticism, especially from the people who call themselves religious, that I determined that it was necessary for me to create a new personality for myself. Over the next few years, I would develop an entirely secular personality that in no way would allow people to look at me with the same skepticism that they had previously.

An incident occurred one day at high school where I needed Dr. Hair's attention. When I saw him, he always called me his Miracle Boy. Marching a company of Junior ROTC cadets back to the school armory earlier that day, four or five other cadet officers, all of higher rank than me, called me from formation to where they were. One of the officers who I thought was my friend distracted me, and suddenly I was sucker punched by another officer. The blow was so severe that I immediately lost awareness of what was happening and was unable to defend myself.

Ruth, my Guardian angel, appeared and led me toward the armory and to the school first aid room. About half way to the armory, I began to realize what had happened. Ruth increased her grip on me and told me to leave it alone. By the time we reached the school's first aid room, Ruth had calmed me. The school nurse attended to my wounds initially and called Mom to come get me and take me to the doctor.

When we arrived at Dr. Hair's office, it was almost empty. The doctor's wife and he were cleaning out the last of his medical equipment and supplies because he had retired. As we started to leave the office, we heard the doctor call out from the back of the clinic.

"Who is that out there?"

The doctor's wife answered that it was Miracle Boy and Iva. The doctor came rapidly to the front office just in time to stop us from going out the door.

"You aren't going anywhere, Miracle Boy. Come on back here, and I'll fix you up."

During the examination, he told me I would require some stitches, but he didn't have anything to deaden the pain. I didn't like that a bit. He wanted to know if I wanted him to take me to the hospital to sew up my cuts. With that question,

I asked how much would it hurt. He told me it would hurt a lot but nothing like the pain I went through with the meningitis.

"Okay," I said. "Let's give it a try."

It hurt a lot, and I wished I had taken him up on going to the hospital.

While he was working on me, he asked about the nurse called Mary. He asked if I thought she was an angel. I was surprised that he knew about her. I told him that I did remember her but asked how he knew about her.

He told me that one day, after I left the hospital, the hospital staff asked him if he knew her and if he knew how they could reach her because they needed to get her paycheck to her. He told them that he didn't know the nurse, that he had only seen her around the hospital when she came to him with questions. The hospital administrator said she gave him as her reference and that they thought he could take her paycheck to her because she disappeared soon after I left the hospital.

There was no doubt in Dr. Hair's mind that I had died and gone to paradise. Standing at my bedside and entering my time of death in the records, he was sure he didn't make any mistakes. He also told me he went back to the ward to have another look at me after he completed his notes at the nurse's station. He wanted to make doubly sure there was no sign of life.

He told me I should go by the Children's Hospital with Mom or Dad and ask for my medical records. He insisted they would give them to me if Mom or Dad accompanied me and signed for them because I was a minor by law. When I asked Mom and Dad to take me to get the records, they refused, saying it was best to forget it ever happened. Dad said it was like a cow pod in the field, the more you stir it the more it stinks, meaning the more I would have to endure when anyone found out about my illness and going to paradise.

High school ended, and as with most young men my age, I was anticipating a greeting letter from Uncle Sam. The draft was alive and well; it was only a matter of time. Not only did I feel alone, I think I *was* alone. Furthermore, there seemed to be no direction in my life. The job I had at Kroger was getting a little stale now that high school had ended, and any other good job couldn't be found because the draft into the military was facing me, possibly only weeks away. It seemed to me, at that time, that if God were really watching out for me, he would have had something ready for me to do. *(He was; I just didn't have enough intelligence, faith, or sensitivity to know it.)* It felt to me as though I was being pushed into military service when it wasn't something I wanted to do. I spent three years in Junior ROTC in high school and discovered, while I was good at doing those military things, it really wasn't something that I wanted to do—especially in the army, because that is where the draft would have placed me. Two of my brothers were in the navy, so I didn't want that, and one brother had served in the army, so I enlisted in the US Air Force. Going into the air force turned out to be one of the best things that happened to me and is a perfect example of being nudged or lightly pushed by God to do what is best for you.

By being in the air force and seeing the way people were in a very close setting, I thought, would be a good time to concentrate on the new personality I was creating. It was during my military service that I took on bad habits such as using profane language, drinking alcohol, carousing with women, fighting, playing cards, and gambling, among many other bad habits. I make no apologies for the habits or for my actions during those years, but in retrospect, I wish I had never engaged in those activities.

The Turning Point

Time spent in the air force gave me the opportunity and confidence to be face-to-face with people I would never have met otherwise. Seeing vulgarity, cruelty, drinking, cursing, smoking, and such a wide range of emotion, behavior, and events was a revelation. My parents sheltered me from these things, and they weren't permitted in our home. In retrospect, that was something I needed in order to help me grow as a man and as an adult. Had my parents exposed me to those types of things and taught how to deal with them, I wouldn't have been as vulnerable. My mental and emotional development at that time was probably equivalent to a thirteen or maybe a fourteen-year-old kid, so I was easy to manipulate. Maybe God saw the air force as the place for me to be exposed to the harsh and evil ways of the world and to develop defenses. Even though some of us came out of the service a bit screwed up, is there a better place to learn more quickly than in the military service?

By the time I enlisted in the air force, my self-confidence and self-esteem were low. During the second week of training in the air force, I, along with all new recruits, engaged in long days of testing. At the end of the testing, each Airman learned his score and what technical schools he was eligible to attend. I was speechless when told my scores were excellent and that I qualified for any available technical school. There was only one catch. Because of a shortage, only one technical school was available, and that was the Weather School at Chanute Air Force Base, Illinois. Therefore, I became a weatherman.

I wasn't happy with that because I desperately wanted to be an aerial photographer. However, I couldn't believe my test results and told the tester there must have been a mistake because everyone had told me I was retarded. The tester told me that I had some of the top scores of all that belonged to my squadron. When I told the tester that my school principal and others were sure I was retarded, he said, "They must be nuts."

That meant either I was in a squadron of real dummies or I wasn't retarded. I walked away from the testing center that day seeing myself in an all-new light.

Wow, could it be that I'm not retarded? I asked myself. On that day, I started standing taller, working harder, and feeling better about myself than I had felt in the past ten years since my illness.

Heaven seldom gets the credit for events in our lives that appear to be a coincidence. We usually attribute the incidents to someone's good nature, humanity, or just being a nice person, when, if we look more closely, God may have had his hand on the event. For example, a number of interesting things happened to me while in the service that I am now convinced were interventions or guidance by God, the Holy Spirit, or Jesus Christ. At the time I thought these were just great people, and I was happy for the helping hand.

New recruits in the air force were paid sixty dollars a month. After deductions, we received around forty-eight dollars to last us all month. Normally that was sufficient because the air force provided all we needed, such as food, lodging, medicine, transportation, etc. However, when we received a three-day pass to leave the base, there wasn't enough money to go very far. It was early in 1957, a few months before my class of recruits was to finish technical school; we were given a three-day pass. It had been quite some time since I had been home to see my family and girlfriend and even though Chattanooga, Tennessee, was beyond the distance limit, I decided to hitchhike home and back.

When dismissed early in the morning, I grabbed my AWOL bag, made it to the east gate of Chanute Air Force Base, put out my thumb, and headed toward Champagne/Urbana, Illinois. My first hitch gave me a ride to the intersection of US-45 and US-150 at Urbana. Walking a few hundred feet east on US-150, holding out my thumb as I walked, it wasn't long before an older looking car drove past me and then stopped maybe a thousand feet ahead of me.

Now, usually someone wanting to give you a lift would back up or motion for you to hurry up. That car, I think it was a 1948 or 1949 four-door Chevrolet or Pontiac, just sat there. At first I continued to walk backward toward the parked car with my thumb out, but as I got closer, I thought the driver might be waiting on me, so I began walking faster toward the car. When I reached the passenger side of the car, the window was down about three or four inches. The driver asked me if I needed a ride. I said yes, reached for the door knob, opened the door, and put my AWOL bag in the floor in front of the front seat, when he said, "Stop. Don't get in; put your stuff in the backseat."

Doing as he requested and now seated in the backseat, he should have driven off down the road, but he didn't. We just sat there for a couple of minutes, and needless to say, I was getting a little nervous, so I grabbed hold of the door knob with my right hand and my AWOL bag with left hand and prepared to bolt from the car if he made a move toward me. There was a consider-able pause before he asked me where I was going, and after I told him, he asked me if I could drive, and when I said yes, he asked me if I had a driv-er's license, and when I again said yes, he told me to wait a minute and I could drive. Instructing me to get out of the car and stand next to the front passenger door until he had gotten out of the driver's seat, he picked up his papers and things he had in the seat with him and moved to the backseat. After he was seated and the back door closed, he said it was okay for me to get in the driver's seat behind the steering wheel.

I pulled the car out onto the highway and began to drive, when he cautioned me not to exceed the speed limit and keep my eyes on the road. It was kind of a strange pick-up encounter, but I was grateful because it began to mist and could soon turn to rain. One thing you didn't want to do is hitchhike in the rain. Who in their right mind wants a wet, soggy person sitting in their car? Moreover, I didn't have any rain gear with me at all, not even an umbrella.

His name may have impressed me if I had ever heard of him, but I hadn't. He introduced himself as Howard Hughes and told me that he owned a machine shop near Chicago that made drill bits—the kind that drilled holes in the ground for wells. I wasn't impressed, because the only point of reference I had of machine shops was when my dad took me with him into the city to a small dirty machine shop that made everyday parts for some of the factories in the area. We had been driving a little while and approaching Danville, Illinois, when he instructed me to turn right onto US-150 south. I reminded him that I was going to Chattanooga, Tennessee, and that I needed to get further east to US-41, where there was more traffic. After he told me that he wanted me to drive longer and that we would intersect US-41 further on down the road, I agreed to turn right and continue on south.

Along the way, we talked occasionally, as he would look up from his work. Looking in the rearview mirror, I could see he was working on some type of drawing that looked like an airplane. When he noticed I was looking at him and his papers in the rearview mirror, he had me turn the mirror so I couldn't see him or the papers.

It was getting to be around midnight when we approached Vincennes, Illinois, when he said he would be going west from there to Saint Louis, Missouri, and then on to Houston, Texas, and that we would part company here. It was raining now, and I wasn't happy about being dumped out on the highway near midnight, but that is the chance you take when you hitchhike. When we arrived at the intersection of US-41, he instructed me to turn onto a local street, and when I asked him where we were going, he said, "To the train station."

It was then I asked him if I could get out of the car now so I wouldn't have to walk back to the highway. He told me the train station wasn't for him but for me, that he wanted to buy me a ticket for driving him so I could catch a train to Chattanooga.

Pulling into the parking lot at the train station, I noticed he was looking over some brochures, and he told me to stay seated while he checked the train schedules. He then told me that he carried train, bus, and airline schedules for everywhere in case he needed them. A train for Chattanooga would be along in about thirty-five to forty-five minutes. He reached over the seat and dropped some money as he told me to buy a first class round-trip ticket to Chattanooga and back to Rantoul, Illinois.

Before I got out of the car, he told me that when I got out of the air force to come to Chicago to his tool and die shop and tell them that Howard Hughes said to give me a job. They would probably ignore me, but I must insist on seeing his number one man. He told me to tell his number one man to check it out with him that he never forgets a face or name.

Three and a half years later (I had returned to Chanute a year earlier to teach in the weather school) as I exited the north gate of Chanute Air Force Base I sat along the side of the road debating with the Holy Spirit whether to go to Chicago or not. By this time, I was well aware of who Howard Hughes was, but not having seen my girlfriend for some time, I decided to ignore the Holy Spirit and go to Chattanooga, spend a few weeks there, then drive back up to Chicago. While at home, I was involved in a head-on collision. A deaf, mute driver pulled across the centerline in front of me. In addition, a recession had set in, and I couldn't find enough money to make it to Chicago. I should have done what the Holy Spirit wanted me to do because occasionally I find myself wondering how it would have turned out if I had turned left at the air base gate instead of heading south to Chattanooga.

As it turned out, my girlfriend married someone else shortly after I left the air force. The inner voice was telling me to go to Chicago, but I didn't listen. If I had listened, at least I wouldn't have been in Chattanooga for the head-on collision.

Perhaps a month or so after my ride with Howard Hughes, I again received a three-day pass and decided to hitchhike home. Early spring had arrived, and the weather was getting better, or so I thought. Again, we were dismissed on Friday morning, and again I grabbed my AWOL bag and headed home. This time I had made it to US-41 heading south when a trucker stopped and asked where I was going. When I told him, he said he was on his way to Bristol, Tennessee, not very far from Knoxville and that I should be able to get a ride easy from there.

Accepting his offer I climbed into the cab and it wasn't long before I was sound asleep. I must have slept a long time before he stopped at a truck stop, and he bought me coconut pie and coffee. The truck stop wasn't recognizable as one I had seen along US-41 before, and when I asked him about it, he said we weren't on US-41, that he was taking another route to Bristol, Tennessee. Later when we reached Corbin, Kentucky, about an hour before sundown, he stopped the truck and made a phone call. When he returned to the truck, he said I had to get out here and that he had to divert to another city.

He pointed out the direction and highway to Bristol, Tennessee and told me to walk through the city square, and I would find the right highway. Getting on to the highway, I walked until I found the highway to Bristol at a fork in the road. At that point, I waited for any vehicle to come along so I could hitch a ride. Around eight o'clock or so, it began to drizzle and turn to a very light sleet. Even though I was wearing my military winter clothes, it was getting very cold. A woman came out of a service station that had been changed into a small restaurant and motel and invited me in for a cup of coffee to warm up. Not having any money, I declined, but she insisted the coffee would be free. With that promise, I followed her into the restaurant. In those days, it was very comforting to encounter anyone that respected a man in uniform because there was a prevailing anti-military sentiment through out the country.

Was this some type of spiritual intervention? In retrospect, I certainly think it was, even though most folks would say that they totally respected the uniform I was wearing and wanted to do something that would help me. Finishing my coffee, I thanked her and was beginning to make my way to the door when an unshaven man asked me come back and sit down. After I turned around, he pointed to a stool near the cash register. Handing me another cup of coffee, he asked me if I was hungry.

"Yes, but I don't have any money," I responded.

He introduced himself as Hal Sanders, whereupon he said for me to sit tight. Within a few minutes, he brought me a thigh portion of a chicken, some mashed potatoes, and a roll. The chicken he placed in front of me didn't look like any chicken my mom or grandma ever served, and when I looked at it somewhat funny, he explained how he cooked it and coaxed me to eat. It didn't take much coaxing to get me to eat, and it was so good. That was the day I was introduced to Kentucky Fried Chicken.

It was somewhat slow that night after nine o'clock, so he and I talked for a long time. Come to find out, he and I knew some of the same people down around the Tennessee/Alabama state line. He told me all about how he wound up in Corbin, Kentucky, where he came from, his wife, family, about his friend Dave Thomas, how Kentucky Fried Chicken came about, how he hoped someday to franchise, and many other personal things such as how he became known as the Colonel.

We talked until around eleven o'clock when he said it was about time to close up and asked if I had some place to stay. I told him no and he said since the rooms in his motel were full, I could spend the night in the restaurant if I didn't mind sleeping in one of the booths or on the floor. I thanked him, and he went away, I thought, to cleanup and close the restaurant. There was a knock at the locked restaurant door.

When he unlocked the door, two elderly people entered, and he introduced me to them. The elderly couple invited me to ride with them to Bristol, Tennessee. They said they were on their way to visit a friend and I could ride with them. We hadn't been on the road long before the wife told me that Mr. Sanders had called them and asked them to drive me to Bristol that he was paying for their gas and motel cost.

It took me until Saturday morning to arrive in Chattanooga, which gave me only one day and night to visit. Early Sunday morning I departed hitchhiking for Chanute AFB. That would be my last trip home until being transferred to Okinawa.

When I left active duty in 1960 with a final discharge in 1962, I had developed confidence in myself, and I had developed a good knowledge and awareness of the world around me. That made me more capable of dealing with life as a man. I look upon those years as the years I caught up, grew up, became a man, and truly became self-supporting.

It was during those years that God showed me his guidance in a more specific manner. When I would find myself in a situation, he was always there whispering in my ear to guide me through the situation. One might say that was my common sense whispering or that was a sense of right and wrong, but I am convinced it was God, through the Holy Spirit, pointing me in the right direction.

However, throughout this period, I was unable to rid myself of my anger with Jesus because he didn't take me back to paradise. Jesus saying that he would add years to my life didn't even register with me until I was in my late forties or fifties. You see, I thought by now Jesus would have let me die. He had several opportunities during the past years to let things happen that would take my life, but he didn't let me die. When I had my first heart attack, I was sure my time had come, but it wasn't going to happen. I waited three days to die before going to the hospital. Jesus not letting me die then made me even angrier with him.

The Seminole Club

Following discharge from the air force, I didn't have very much luck working for other people. Of course it was my fault; I came back from the military a bit screwed up, like many other servicemen. Apparently I had become, what appeared to be, too arrogant and too opinionated. John Reece was manager of a new Kroger store when I returned to civilian life, and he graciously made a place for me. I wasn't the person John had known before, and working at Kroger was a bit difficult I think for John as well as me. Neither did it help that one of my older brothers was now my immediate boss. Afterward, I tried several other jobs with the same fate. Was it me, or was God leading me to a position where one of Jesus's promises could be kept? As much as I would like to think it was God working in my life, I think in this case it was definitely me.

After losing several jobs, a contract was offered to me by Crabtree Transfer and Storage to drive a semi-tractor-trailer across the country for Allied Van Lines, a national moving company. I accepted the contract, went out, leased a rig, and after two days of training qualified for my ICC licenses. For most of the year, I was alone in the cab of that truck thinking about what I had become. In this case, I think God did have his hand in the pot. Facing oneself and seeing what you really are can be an unsettling time or it can be a character building time. In any case, at the end, you cannot come out the same as you were when the time alone began.

The year long contract was ending just as I was returning from a trip to California and other West Coast locations. I couldn't wait until I could begin anew and re-enter life with a new attitude. Dropping the trailer at the warehouse, I decided to stop by a local watering hole on my way home for some refreshment and a sandwich. Running into an old friend, he invited me to a party at a local university where he said we could let off a little steam, maybe find an agreeable girl, so I agreed to go to the party. After all, I had been on the road for a full year without any companionship at all. The party was well attended, and it was loaded with good-looking college girls looking for a good time and to let off a little steam. It was at this party I met two guys looking to rent a house together, and since they seemed to get along well with me, they asked me if I wanted to join them. The year that I was on the road, all my belongings were at Mom and Dad's house. I was going to have to find my own place, so the idea did catch my attention. However, at first I was leery of moving in with two guys, let alone ones I had just met at a party. I said I would think about it and get together with them in a few days. Several days later we met, and the two guys laid out what they were thinking and also gave me some background information such as where they worked, went to school, etc.

The plan was to rent a large house and transform it into a party house by painting and decorating, putting in a good sound system, and dedicating one room to dancing. The main purpose was of course to entice women to party in a good atmosphere where they would be safe. Good plan, we all agreed, and began looking for a nice house. We called it the Seminole Club. When you opened the front door and looked in, the first thing you saw was a magnum of Old Crow, a dozen shot glasses sitting on the foyer table, and a large picture of a Seminole Indian hanging on the wall above the magnum of Old Crow. It wasn't a real club; we just called it one to impress the girls. Every Friday through Sunday evening, a party was in full swing. Each of us bachelors living there were salesmen, meeting many people each day. As a practice we kept our eye out for attractive women and invited them to the party. To make sure the parties weren't all women, we also invited some men. Don't get me wrong; we never invited as many men as we did women. What would be the point? Several couples were united as a result of meeting someone at the party. Even one of our bachelors bit the dust by getting married.

Remember the vision shown to me about my future wife? Well, when I saw the vision, she would have been less than one year old. Nineteen years later, I would meet her, and she was exactly as I saw her in the vision, except the child was missing.

Returning home from a business trip to Atlanta, I opened the front door to The Seminole Club and walked into the foyer. Looking toward the living room, I was stunned. There she was, just as I had seen many times in my visions.

I had actually met her ten years earlier, when she was nine years old. I vividly remember the meeting because I was puzzled when I saw her. I was puzzled because she looked like someone I should know, but I didn't recognize her as the woman in my vision. However, I did tell my dad as we were leaving—we had delivered a dining room set to her parents—that I had the strangest feeling of being married to that nine-year-old girl to which Dad responded, "Don't be in too big a hurry for that."

She too remembered our first meeting as recognizing something about me that was puzzling and unforgettable.

There was no doubt, except in the visions shown to me, there was a little girl standing at her side. Even though I recognized her as the woman in my visions, I was elated that no little girl was there, and I thought to myself that I could be mistaken. For me to be mistaken would have been great. I was having a ball with all the women and parties and was looking forward to many more and for this woman to be the one in my vision would ruin it.

Standing there staring at her, who should appear in my face? Ruth, my guardian angel. "Well go ahead, your party days are over," she said, and with a nudge I made my way to her.

She was talking to another man when I walked up, so I asked the other man to move along.

Looking at the woman, I said, "If I were to want to contact you, what would be your name and phone number?"

I thought this rude and direct approach would anger her and she would tell me to get lost, but she didn't. She actually gave me her name and phone number. If this was truly the girl in my vision that meant she was the one God had picked out for me, and to refuse would be to refuse God. Although, I have often wondered whether God had picked out the girl for me, or did he just know what decision I would make and was showing me what my decision would be? I had only one hope; there was no kid in sight. We made a date and when I arrived at her house to pick her up; there was the kid exactly as shown to me in the vision.

I was shocked and knew at that moment my bachelor days were numbered. My only way out was to treat her with such bad manners, generally be a jerk, and hopefully she would break it off with me and I would be free without me rejecting God. I tried, but she stuck. We got married about six months later and have been married for more than forty-five years.

Ignoring God

During the next six decades, heaven's presence continued to enter my earthly life intermittently, offering me opportunities to benefit from its perspective, which I didn't always find myself willing to do. I sometimes made myself learn about life in harder ways.

In 1968, Gwen and I had been trying to conceive for more than two years without success. On the night of conceiving our younger daughter, God sent to me a vision of a lovely young woman with blonde hair and an uncanny resemblance to my mother in looks, actions, and philosophy of life. Sure enough, when my daughter, Christinna Richelle, was born I realized the vision was right on; she resembles her grandmother in most respects. Rolling over, I told my wife she had just conceived and to get pencil and paper. I wanted her to write it down. In her nightstand was a green address book and pen. She wrote the date and time, as that was the night of conception. At first she resisted, then reluctantly she did as I asked. After the date and time, I gave her a description of what our daughter would look like. About six weeks later, after the rabbit died, my wife went back and looked at the book. She couldn't believe what she had written. Nine months later, guess what.

Following my first heart attack, Ruth, my guardian angel, walked into the hospital room where I was recovering; I recognized her immediately. She told the doctor she would wait until he was finished talking with me to give me a shot.

After the doctor left the room she told me not to worry, that it was only saline solution. Before she gave the injection to me, she took my hand, and when she did, I felt this warmth and stimulation engulf my entire body, and my pain dissipated. After which, she gave me the injection of saline solution and began a lecture. She said that for too long I had been angry with Jesus Christ for leaving me here so long that I must rid myself of the anger, or I would be back with more and more heart attacks. She insisted it was the anger that caused my heart attack. She explained to me how I should go about eliminating the anger, plus many other things for me to think about, and I began trying to work on how I could rid myself of the anger. It took three more heart attacks and a pacemaker before I would rid myself of the anger. Occasionally my temper will surface, especially when confronted with morons or bad drivers, but never at Jesus. What a joy it is to finally be at peace; my family says I am a lot nicer to be around, and that's a good thing.

In 2000, my wife and I were planning a six-month RV vacation across the country. We were to travel up the east coast, across the northern tier of the States, down along the West Coast, and then east along the southern border, and on to our home in Florida. About a week before we were to leave, I began getting the impression from God that all of our investments and retirement fund were in jeopardy and the stocks we owned should be sold. That didn't make a lot of sense to me; the market was doing great, and all of the brilliant people were saying don't sell; keep investing. *Greed is a terrible thing. It couldn't be God telling me to sell; it must have been Satan whispering in my ear so we wouldn't make as much money,* I thought. *Why should I jeopardize our earnings by selling the stock?* So I didn't sell. That wouldn't be the first time that old Satan had impersonated God to get me to do something that wasn't good for me. Later, I discussed this with my wife and her response was, "Don't sell since we've done really well. We need to make as much as we possibly can, so why upset the apple cart."

We loaded our RV and departed for our trip, leaving the stocks secure in the bank safety deposit box.

As anyone owning stock remembers, the stock market began crashing that year. Unfortunately, we were on vacation, many miles from home, when it began; and no, we didn't watch the news or read the papers. We were on *vacation*. When we heard about the market crashing, we cut our vacation short, but by the time we returned home to sell our stock certificates, we had lost 80 percent of the value of our retirement fund. Again, yes, I know the certificates should have been taken to a broker before we departed on our vacation so I could use telephone to tell them to sell, but I didn't do that. I know it was stupidity on my part because God was telling me to sell the stocks for my own good, but because of greed, I thought Satan was fooling with me. Over the years I have often mixed knowing whether it is God or Satan telling me what to do; this was no different.

Lucifer is the great imposter, which is why he is called by so many names. He was an imposter in the Garden of Eden, and he has been deceiving humanity for millennia. I'll bet Lucifer, that old Satan, has deceived you too and you blamed God when you should have blamed Satan.

My Family Sees Paradise

At age thirty-seven, Jesus Christ spoke to me several times telling me that if I didn't change my ways, he was going to have to kill me and take me home. Actually, dying and going back to heaven was good news to me, except for a little problem. That problem was threefold. One was five years old, blonde haired and beautiful; and the second was eleven years old, dark brown-haired beautiful girl; and, of course, my wife. They were my purpose for living, and I loved them with every ounce of love I had. I couldn't die and leave them without me in their lives. After all, they all were gifts shown to me in one vision while I was in paradise and the other shown to me in a vision twenty-three years after I returned from paradise. Can any man be more blessed?

From the moment Jesus Christ told me he was going to kill me if I didn't change my ways, I began trying to change back to follow his direction rather than my own. No more drinking, gambling, profanity, and staying away from church for me. (I've done real well with everything except for that pesky profanity thing. On occasion out will pop a word left better unsaid). When I said "I do" at the altar, I meant it and, although I still love to look at beautiful women, Gwen has been the only woman in my life. Oh, yes, there were many opportunities and much temptation, but with the help of the angels, I have been able to honor my wedding vows. (Lets face it; a man that doesn't honor his wedding vows has no honor at all). I am still alive, so I must have pleased Jesus enough for him to leave me here for my family.

It was during this period of returning to Jesus that my father called me late one night around bedtime and said he was having chest pains and difficulty breathing. I asked him to please call for an ambulance since I was quite a distance from him. He said no. He wanted me to come out to him, and I said, "I will, but first I am going to call and get an ambulance on its way."

He said, "Don't do that because I won't go with them, and I'll be angry with you, so please get here as quickly as you can."

Having already undressed and prepared for bed, I rushed to get my clothes on and get to the motel where he was working. When I got to him, he was having severe pains and difficulty breathing. Deciding it would take too long for an ambulance to get there, I put him in the front seat of my car and headed toward the hospital.

The first hospital refused to take him because they said they had no one on duty and the emergency room was closed. We had to drive several miles to another hospital that did have an active emergency room. I was trying to get him out of the car and to the emergency room when several nurses with a wheelchair came running toward him. They had almost reached him when he took his last breath and collapsed to the ground. By then a team had arrived, and they managed to get him onto a gurney and rush him into the emergency room. They wouldn't let me see him for a while as they worked on him. The nurse told me that his heart had completely stopped and that they were trying to resuscitate him.

In about an hour, they came to me and told me that they had managed to resuscitate him and he was in the critical care unit under constant watch. They allowed me to go to the unit and see him. He was so under the influence of medication all that I could do was talk to him and hope he understood. He didn't even respond, but I could see his eyes move, and I was satisfied that he would pull through. The doctors told me there was nothing else I could do and for me to go home and that by morning he should be awake enough to be able to recognize me.

On the way to work the next morning, I went by the hospital to see him in the critical care unit, and he was still asleep. I didn't have the heart to awaken him, so I left and went on to work. That evening on the way home, I again stopped at the hospital, and he was more awake but not too coherent. The nurse said he was doing well and that I should not disturb him for more than one or two minutes, so I didn't. Most of the time at each visit was spent talking with Mom and trying to give her as much comfort as possible.

The next morning when I went to the hospital to see him, they told me they had moved him to a room. I found his room, and when I went through the door and saw him lying on his side, there was this big smile on his face like I have never seen. As I approached the bed, with eyes beaming and his face aglow, he looked at me in a way he had never looked at me before. He simply said, "I saw the twins."

I said, "Twins? Have Douglas and Donald been here?"

He said, "No, the no-name twins that died." And he said, "I gave them names. After I gave them names, they told me I needed to come back, and here I am. Son, I am so sorry for doubting you all those years about what you said and about going to paradise."

A little later, when Mother arrived at the hospital, he asked if they could be alone for a few minutes.

I said, "Dad, you are passing gas like a steam engine. Are you sure you want Mom to stay?"

He said, "Son, it isn't the first time she heard that, so go outside for a little bit."

After a while I cracked open the door to the hospital room and looked in. They were both crying. Mother was leaning over the bed. They were hugging, and I don't know when I have seen them happier. Dad had told her about seeing Ralph and the twins and giving the twins names. There was no reason for them to blame each other anymore for the babies' deaths.

From that day until the day my father passed away several years later, I never heard them raise their voice in anger or say an unkind word to each other. They were like two kids on a honeymoon, and I thought if only all people who lose a child could see what my father saw, they would be so much happier.

Sometime during the 1980s, an issue arose between my siblings and me. Reluctantly, and under the influence of her husband, my sister joined with my brothers to commit an act that was very offensive to me. The nature of that act isn't important. What is important is that it caused an estrangement between them and me for many years. It was during that period that somewhere in Illinois my younger brother suffered a massive heart attack at a truck stop while eating dinner.

Sometime after he recovered from the heart attack he managed to get a load to deliver in Florida. On that day a telephone call came into the office while I was away. Upon my return my executive assistant said my younger brother was waiting to see me at a Friday's restaurant on US-50. I thanked her for the message and went into my office.

About an hour later she came in and urged me to go see him because he said he could only wait until sundown for me. I am ashamed to say that I never went to see him. A few years later, his heart failed to where it was necessary for him to go on disability. Within two years he died. Before he died, one of my other brothers begged me to come to the hospital in Tennessee to see him. It wasn't until my sister urged me to at least talk with him on the phone that we did communicate. I told him I forgave him and for him to enjoy his journey to paradise. I know, I was a real jerk, but at that time it really hurt to even think about being in the presence of my siblings. Through the urging of my family, we did attend his internment and then departed to visit my Mom in the nursing home.

At Mom's funeral, I faced my two remaining siblings. I promised to bury the hatchet since Mother was now in paradise and the offense against her would be forgiven and forgotten. Since then, we have grown close together and now have a relationship as brothers should have. I have told you all of this to tell you what they told me that day about our younger brother that would shake me immensely. They told me the reason our younger brother waited so long in Orlando to see me was that he had gone to paradise and returned when he had the heart attack in Illinois and wanted me to know that he now understood. Unfortunately, I missed a moment in time that can never be recaptured with my younger brother.

Several years passed, and again I became victim of my own arrogant failure to care for my health, just as do many men and women. We choose to take care of business, work, or family instead of taking time to see or follow up with the doctor when feeling ill. A mid- to late-1980s examination revealed polyps in my colon. A follow-up with the specialist confirmed the diagnosis, and I made an appointment to have them removed. However, I didn't keep the appointment because the doctor wouldn't accommodate my schedule.

September 1996, one week after my business sold, I decided to go to the doctor for a physical checkup. It was at that checkup the doctor ordered additional testing, including a colonoscopy for me. I had put off having a colonoscopy for many years because the first sigmoidoscopy in late 1980s was so painful, and I knew what they would find. Well, I was just about to pay the price for that false pride. With grumbling, and after the new type of procedure was explained to me,

I suffered the indignity and made my way to the gastroenterologist. I thought it would be somehow manlier to joke about it in an attempt to cover up my disdain for this procedure.

Waking up from the procedure, I was ready to go home, but the doctor had other ideas. The doctor asked my wife and me to meet him in his conference room, saying that he wanted to review the results of the test. My wife fell like a falling tree when the doctor showed us the test results. I had a cancerous tumor the size of a grapefruit near the descending portion of my colon, and it was growing rapidly. Radical treatment was the only answer.

"So, does this mean that if I don't have the treatment, I will die?" I asked.

With a very serious look on his face, the doctor told me that without treatment, I would be dead in six months, and even with the treatment, I shouldn't expect to live more than two years. My wife was devastated and in tears. I was taking the diagnosis lightly and that troubled the doctor. He suggested my wife and I consider the test results and get back to him in two days.

Not much was said between Gwen and me as we drove back home. When we reached home, I immediately said I was going into my office to look at some stuff. What I was really going to do was begin arranging for my death because I had no intention of having the cancer treatments. Both my daughters were grown women and doing well for themselves, and for over fifty years, I had looked forward to the time when I would get to go back to paradise, and I wasn't going to let this opportunity pass.

I seemed too happy around the house the rest of the day. Every time Gwen wanted to talk about the cancer, I changed the subject. She asked me over and over when I was going to arrange to have the treatments. Finally, I broke down and told her that I wasn't going to have any treatments or operation. With anger and fear, she asked why not.

"This is my chance to go back to paradise, and I'm not going to miss the opportunity," I blurted out, without thinking about the repercussions.

"What do you mean?" she asked. "You can't be serious. You want to die?"

I had told her nothing about dying. My wife only knew what my sister had told her when we visited them in St. Louis twenty-five years earlier and about the family praying me back from death. She didn't believe my sister, so it was easy to avoid the subject. I thought my wife had forgotten about what my sister said. Gwen insisted I sit with her and tell her what had happened when I was seven almost eight. That did nothing to ease her sorrow. I think it made it worse. She pleaded for her sake and the sake of the children to have the operation and take the treatments.

I stood fast until the next day when my youngest daughter called from California. I had two daughters—one adopted and one I had fathered naturally. My daughters had broken through my rigid layer of resistance. They pleaded with me and told me how much they needed me asking how could I leave them when there was a chance I would survive? No longer could I resist and agreed to have the operation and treatments.

I thought a lot about the doctor saying I would have about two years to live with the operation and treatments. It wouldn't be right to leave my wife alone to take care of the big house we lived in so I purchased a lot in a condominium subdivision on a golf course. It was to be my wife's widow home. The house would be small enough for her to handle and large enough that she wouldn't feel lost and the condominium association would fully maintain the house and property for her. Before cancer, she had said she wouldn't want to live in the big house without me.

Waking up from the surgery and hearing a female voice, the only question I asked was, "Am I dead?"

The answer was, "No, you aren't dead."

I responded, "Well, shit," and went back to sleep.

Even though the operation and treatments went well, I was beginning to accept that I would be here longer and that I should make the best of my time. Life was good for a couple of years, when I noticed blood in my stools when I went to the bathroom. First, came anger, then came depression and then came a silent contentment within me.

The second cancer was much more aggressive than the first. It had invaded my sacrum, and every physician that examined me deemed it inoperable. The surgeon that removed my first cancer recalled reading an article authored by one of his friends at the Mayo Clinic. His friend had attempted removing a cancer similar to mine. His patient survived a couple years after the operation but was paralyzed. The surgeon pleaded with his friend at the Mayo Clinic for help. Finally, the Mayo Clinic offered an opportunity for me in a program that had no guarantees of success. Even with the treatments, the program only gave me a twenty percent chance of survival with no possibility of living another couple years. Because of the cancer's location, I would probably be permanently paralyzed from the waist down. That is, if the treatments were successful.

Radiation and chemotherapy were about to begin when I received a call that my sister was in the hospital and her full recovery was very doubtful. Her body had began to reject her kidney transplant, and some other internal organs were showing signs of failing. The doctors at the Mayo Clinic insisted the treatment on me begin immediately; however, my sister was the only person that really believed I went to paradise, and I wasn't about to abandon her as she faced the end of her life on earth. A few months before her admission into the hospital, while visiting with her at her home, she called me into her bedroom. She reminded me of the day her son fell from a tree into some high-tension power lines and was electrocuted. The emergency medical team was working with him on the ground as he struggled to stay alive. Remembering how the family prayed me back, she left his side and called me on the telephone. She questioned me about the details of paradise and whether we should let him go or try to pray him back. After explaining exactly what would happen to him there, she asked me if I would want to be prayed back if I were him. I told her that I wasn't him and that I couldn't speak for him, but if I was, praying me back would be the last thing I would want you to do. Byron passed on shortly thereafter.

While we were alone together, she again asked me to tell her about paradise. And afterward, she was very relaxed and at peace with possibility of dying. She also asked me to do her one last favor. Her husband, Gene, also believed the family had prayed me back to earth. Earlene was afraid he would try to pray her back, and she asked me to promise that I wouldn't take part in that effort—that if I felt comfortable with doing it, to intercede with God and ask him to ignore any attempt to pray her back. Sure enough, after she passed away, her family tried desperately to pray her back, but God chose to honor Earlene's wishes over her family's wishes.

During the week after my sister's internment, the preacher that conducted the services came to me and wanted to talk about paradise. He told me that his mother had a similar experience and that because she came back, it seemed to him that God had rejected her. After considerable conversation, I think he was convinced that wasn't the case. We come back to earth for one of two reasons. First, we can be jerked back by some medical procedure, or we come back because God asks or allows us to return for a purpose. In his mother's case, it was very clear she needed to perform a service for Jesus Christ, and she did; then she died.

One week after Mom's internment, we were at the same funeral home for Sister's internment service. There is no proof, nor is there any way

I can point to anything significant, but I have always felt that God allowed Mom to pass and to honor Earlene's wishes so Mom would be there to greet her in paradise when she arrived. I still feel that same way even today.

The treatments for my cancer had been put off for a little over a month, and the cancer had grown considerably. Anyone who has undergone radiation and chemotherapy knows just how horrible the treatments are. The treatments continued for the next three months; I think the radiation and chemotherapy treatments were worse than the cancer. They installed a pump into my arm that injected chemo directly into my heart twenty-four hours a day, seven days a week. My hair fell out; blisters came up on my skin, and my mouth and digestive track was so blistered that I could only eat ice cream. Don't get me wrong. I love ice cream. That was the good part. The doctors at the Mayo Clinic nearly panicked when my sugar level shot through the roof. In addition, twice a day for thirty-seven days, my wife drove me to the clinic for radiation treatments.

As the treatments were winding down at the Mayo Clinic, the lead doctor on the team informed me that the operation could only be accomplished at the Rochester, Minnesota, clinic. That was one of only four places in the United States that had the equipment needed for the operation, they told me. The clinic wanted me to fly to Minnesota. They would make the airplane and hotel reservations, but my wife had another idea. We could take our motor home so we would have a familiar place to recover after the operation. They questioned the wisdom of driving fifteen hundred miles after my treatments, but my wife assured them that she would drive while I rested in the bed.

Time had come to say what might be my last good-byes to my family and friends. My brothers, brother-in-law, relatives, and children made their way to our house. Both of my remaining brothers volunteered to drive us to Rochester, but my wife insisted she could make the trip own her own. All of my affairs were in order. I made sure my wife knew everything I knew about our affairs and about handling my portion of the family affairs. We had the small house on the golf course, so I knew she could move there if I didn't survive the operation. My relatives were great. But before they helped us prepare the motor home and made sure our house was secure, they wanted to have a prayer circle. Just like the one they had when I was seven years old and declared dead except we would be standing because they knew how painful it would be for me to kneel.

You can say all you want to about God's healing powers for individuals being a myth, but I know better. There are preachers out there telling people they can cast out demons, heal the sick, and do all kinds of wonders in the name of Jesus Christ and God. I don't know about those folks; are they for real or not? They must be as skeptical about me as I am about them and probably as skeptical as you are about me. That isn't what I am talking about. My brothers, children, and some in-laws circled around me and placed their hands on my body and began to pray. At first, one at a time, then after each had prayed individually, they began to pray in unison. There was no specific kind of feeling that I had at that moment, but during that period, I was sure Jesus Christ was listening to their prayers. No one can convince me otherwise.

With all the loose ends tied, my wife and I got in our motor home and began the long journey to the Mayo Clinic in Rochester, Minnesota. The trip was exhausting. I was very weak from the chemotherapy and radiation. Setting up a motor home at a campground can be difficult, in any weather. It was now late-October in Minnesota and cold. Some of the other campers at the RV park helped my wife by doing most of the work setting up our campsite. The next morning we made our way to the Mayo Clinic Hospital for my operation. God couldn't have picked a better doctor to be the lead physician than Dr. Heidi Nelson. She was a small-framed woman, and I took to her immediately. What a marvelous person. We talked extensively about the operation. She wanted to make sure I fully understood the nature of the surgery and the remote possibilities of survival. If I survived, it would be for only a short time, maybe six months, maybe in the long shot, two years.

In any event, I would probably be paralyzed from the waist down because she didn't see any way the tumor could be removed from around the sacrum without possibly damaging the nerves in the spine. I told her that between you and me, it wouldn't hurt at all if you happened to slip during the operation and cut an artery and let me bleed to death. She didn't like that at all.

I had to ask. After all, I'd been waiting with anticipation for the angel of death to come calling for almost five decades. Not because I'm tired of living or suicidal, nor because I'm unhappy with my life, family, or accomplishments. No, I simply await the angel of death because I know what awaits me in paradise. I couldn't help thinking, *Maybe I will die during this operation.*

That was more than thirteen years ago, and I'm still here.

God Speaks

Rather often, when I tell my wife something, she will roll her eyes up into her head and say something like that's nice, dear. If anyone else has had this type of death experience, you know, one similar to mine and if they told anyone about the experience, I'll wager whomever they told thought they were nuts. You know, sort of like telling some you have been abducted by aliens.

Let me tell you about one of many experiences that, even today, my wife cannot understand. One Sunday morning in the mid-nineties, after we had eaten breakfast, we sat down into the living room to read the Sunday newspaper. While she was separating the newspaper sections, I sat there debating whether to tell her what I saw while asleep the night before. First I asked her if she believed anyone could leave their body while asleep and fly around the countryside and go anywhere they desired.

I got the usual, "Yeah, right. Dreaming again, are we?"

On the previous Saturday night, I wasn't unusually tired or troubled. Dinner was bland, lightly-spiced easy foods to digest that always agree with me, and it had been more than thirty years since any significant amount of alcoholic beverage had crossed my lips. Over the years I hadn't been able to correlate any of this type of an event to anything that would give indication it was caused by something I did or didn't do, eat or drink.

Around one o'clock Sunday morning, I came out of my body, turned around, looked at my body and wife in the bed, and then I flew out through the closed window and into the night. It was a beautiful night, full of stars and with a slight coolness in the air—a kind of romantic night you dream about, maybe holding the hand of your love and walking along the beach. I was thinking, *This is the most wonderful place in the world to be.* Zooming out over Lake Griffin, Tavares, and orange groves (I could smell their fragrance), I headed south. The Disney World area was my destination. As I reached the Florida Turnpike, all traffic was stopped because of a terrible accident. Hovering over the accident, I witnessed angels taking the spirits of the dead toward heaven. Chills and agony engulfed me as I saw a couple of Lucifer's angels taking the souls of two people. I had no problem recognizing them as Lucifer's angels, because some of them I had seen on my way to paradise. One of the souls was the driver of the semi-truck, and I didn't get to see where the other person came from. Leaving the scene of the accident, I was suddenly yanked back to my body. As I came through the closed window toward my body, I saw my wife shaking my body, yelling, "Breathe, breathe!"

Jumping into my body, I took a gulping breath of air, and she said, "Thank God."

That wasn't the first time she had shaken me when she found me not breathing. Assuming it was some sort of sleep disorder, I never told her any different until that day. After telling her what I had seen, as usual, she thought I had dreamed all of it. With that, I asked her to turn on the television to a station that has local news.

When the news came on, the lead story was about the wreck on the Florida Turnpike.

Out of her mouth came, "Oh my God! Is that what you were just telling me about?"

"Yes," I responded.

With that she said, "Maybe you didn't dream it after all; I don't know how you knew about it, but it sounds really weird to me."

After that Sunday morning when I told her I dreamed something, she always asked if it was like the turnpike accident or what.

I have never heard of this kind of thing happening to anyone else. If someone had just told this to me, I would have thought they were in the twilight zone. The next thing I would expect to hear is that they had seen space aliens while they were flying around. Well, I've never seen any space aliens anywhere, and whether they exist or not, I don't know or really care.

Unfortunately, relating this kind of experience to anyone brings on an extreme amount of skepticism, as it should. There are fabricators of stories and events around by the thousands, maybe millions and each case should be met with doubt and skepticism. How often have you heard someone say "God told me…" or God has shown me…" or something similar?

Does God talk to you? How do you know when God is communicating with you? Those are excellent questions, and for me they are difficult questions to answer. I think the question should be phrased, "How does heaven talk to you, and how do you know when heaven is communicating with you?"

There is more than one way that heaven communicates with me. Sometimes God (our heavenly Father) or Jesus Christ will communicate with me directly, which occurs seldom, or heaven will send instruction via the Holy Spirit or the angels. I hear most often from the Holy Spirit. Coming directly from the angels is the easiest to recognize because sometime they make themselves visible. Sometimes there is a faint impression about what I should do or how I should go or how I should act. Some might say this is nothing more than my conscience or common sense talking. They may be right, but those impressions have never been wrong, and I think if it was my conscious or common sense, there would occasionally be something that didn't work. In any event, no matter what channel is used to communicate heavenly messages to you, one thing is for sure: they all come from God, our heavenly Father. The important thing isn't how a message arrives, but that we listen to the message.

On occasion, I have been extremely stubborn about listening to God because of the situation that I was in at the moment. When that happens, sometimes God seems to yell at me in an audible voice—similar to the voice I heard on the mountain that sent me to the revival when I was seven years old.

I ignored most of what heaven was telling me during and after my military service because I figured I could well depend on myself and that I didn't need God's help. Then he got my attention. During the early 1970s, while at work, God spoke to me in an audible way: "Go home and get some rest."

That didn't make any sense to me because I wasn't tired, had a lot of work to do, and felt good. For some reason, that day I listened, put my tools down, and went home around one o'clock in the afternoon. When I got home, my wife asked me why I was there when I should have been at work. I told her what God had said to me, and she shrugged and sarcastically said, "Well, then I guess you had better go to bed, huh?"

Moreover, that is exactly what I did. I went to bed, and I went to sleep.

Late that evening, the telephone rang, and as the telephone rang, I had a vision of my brother Douglas being crush by a backhoe. My wife entered the bedroom with the phone in hand; she was as white as sheet, with a slight trembling in her voice. Douglas had been crushed and killed by a backhoe. The next twenty-four hours would be sleepless hours because of the things that I had to do for the family and for my brother. God had sent me home preparing me for this event, and I knew it. I began to realize that I really needed to pay more attention to what God was saying and to be careful what I dismissed.

In the mid-1970s, my wife and I found ourselves in the difficult position of being jobless and broke. We didn't even have any food in the refrigerator.

We came to be in this predicament after my small construction business failed. Wanting to provide our prospective customers with a wider choice at a lower cost meant reselling a manufactured item. Until then we had built all of our projects by hand from the ground down, you might say. Our business was swimming pools and the like.

On that day, we had unloaded a semi-truck load of pools and supplies. There were so many products they were stacked to the ceiling. My younger brother was in charge of the warehouse's goods for safekeeping. Heavy rains and winds began to arrive just before closing time, and he was in a hurry to leave and go home. Unfortunately, he failed to turn off the lights when he left. Unknown to me at the time, he had allowed boxes to be stacked too close to the light fixtures in the ceiling. My wife greeted me when I arrived home with phone in hand; it was the fire department. Our warehouse was on fire. The losses we suffered were so severe that insurance covered only a portion of the loss. We kept the business together as long as possible, but it was an uphill, losing battle. We sold our home and took the little amount of money from the sale and moved to Orlando, Florida, and took over the payments on a home owned by another veteran. We managed for a few months without finding work, but soon the money ran out. There was nothing left for me to do but to go begging or go to the federal government or state government or county government and ask for charity.

I drove to the parking lot where the government office handed out food stamps. The closer I came to the door of the government office, the shakier I got, and the more difficult it was for me to place one foot in front of the other. One might say I was just scared. Okay, I won't discount or take issue with that, but I have never been afraid to walk into an office or to present myself in front of someone. It turns out I am one of those pushy type-A personalities that just doesn't mind marching in and making their presence known. This was an unusual feeling for me; it had never happened before. All I could hear in my head was, *Go home; I will take care of you.* Stopping, I listened to the voice and removed my hand from the door, turned around, and started walking toward the car, and as I did, all of the feelings I was having left me, and I felt comforted. At home, I notice the mail had arrived. In the mail was a sizable check—more than enough to fill the refrigerator, pay all our bills, and carry us for a few weeks longer.

Long ago I had forgotten about a debt owed to me. In fact, it was written off long ago as a bad debt on our taxes. We moved soon after our business collapsed and had given our new address to only a few relatives and our lawyer. How the person that owed us the money found us is still a mystery.

There was less than one hundred dollars left from the check when one evening, I received a call from my neighbor down the street. He knew of our circumstances and had asked around at his employer if they had any openings where they could use me. There was a position in their construction estimating department that I could interview for. The interview was arranged, and before nightfall they called me with a job offer. Was this God inspired or just the actions of a good neighbor? You be the judge. All I can say is that the job seemed to fall in my lap, at just the right time, with the right amount of pay to keep us going.

On another occasion, I was earmarked for a promotion. I wanted the promotion. I was extremely looking forward to the promotion. The message from God was, "Don't take the promotion," which I shrugged off. Over the next hour, he repeated the warning until it got to the point where I was shaking and couldn't concentrate on my work. Leaving my office, I walked to the head of the division's office and told him to please remove my name from consideration. Talk about tough; that was one of the most difficult tasks I ever had to perform. Within days, I received an offer for employment with a contractor that almost doubled my income and prestige. Was God looking out for me?

Lately I have been reflecting on how my association with heaven has affected me inwardly and how the relationship has affected me on an inner personal basis. God touches everyone's life—saint and sinner, believer or unbeliever. It is like when the rain falls; it has no regard for the differences between the good or the bad, the white or the black, the red or the yellow, righteous or unrighteous, saint or sinner, rich or poor, or anything else you can think of. However, those who believe and have been redeemed will receive additional effects on their life in the form of answered prayers, healing, or other blessings. Maybe that isn't the correct way to explain it;

maybe the only effect that really matters is in the afterlife. Of course, many will say that an afterlife doesn't exist. Well dummy, the joke is on you. I have been there, and I know better.

There is no doubt; there is no question in my mind, and even though there were times that I thought God was taking a vacation, he was touching my life. Maybe you can say the same thing. I am sure there are many such people around this world that can testify to a personal relationship with God, where they can say unequivocally God has touched their life. The touching can be almost like a whisper or maybe a slight nudge, or maybe all avenues seem closed except one.

An inner relationship with God I have found to be not much different to a good relationship with a good dad. It takes an effort on both sides to form a good relationship; it cannot come from one side only. If we do our part, we can always count on our dad for his part. A good dad always gives a son good advice, not orders, and a helping hand along with a word of guidance, support, and sometimes comfort. Having the knowledge of knowing that you can always depend on your dad no matter what is exactly how I came to realize what kind of relationship I had with God. It is a very personal relationship. It is a relationship that I cannot even begin to describe; you simply know and understand what it is. I am no one special; there are millions of people in this world who have that type of relationship with God, so it isn't unusual. I suppose the only people that will think it is unusual are those who have never had the good fortune to have that kind of a relationship with their dad or with God.

Remember Ninevah

When you hear the name Nineveh, how can you not recall the story about Jonah and the whale? Regardless of whatever religious group, order, or church a person is connected to, if any at all, at one time or the other, almost everyone has heard the story of Jonah and the whale, or more correctly, the big fish. That is one of the stories told most often as a children's story and as an adult example of obedience to God. This chapter isn't about the story of Jonah or about the whale or big fish, but it is about how heaven has kicked my butt to get on with these writings. Let me make it clear how I feel about having to write about these things. Again, writing this book and making this information available to anyone is something I didn't want to do. For more than a decade and a half, I prayed asking God to relieve me of the burden to expose these things. The stronger the impression was to write this book, the more I resisted. I didn't want anyone to know what happened to me as a child and the effect it had on me as an adult. It's no one's business but mine, and I'll be put-upon by the naysayers and critics and misquoted by many. It'll surprise me if the theologians aren't the most brutal in their criticisms, and that is how it should be, but it'll not be their fault. That is the way they were educated and the convictions they hold. Through my entire life, I have refused to read any books or articles on this subject because I didn't want my memories to be corrupted, tainted, or contaminated.

There is a paradise, and there is a heaven. On occasion, I have heard some people refer to paradise as the first heaven and heaven as the second heaven. I use the word paradise because of what Jesus Christ told the thief on the cross next to him:

> And he said unto Jesus, Lord, remember me when thou comest into thy kingdom.
> And Jesus said unto him, Verily I say unto thee, Today shalt thou be with me in paradise.
>
> Luke 23:42–43 (KJV)

And that is what it is called by the angels. While in paradise, a portion of heaven was shown to me, but none of the redeemed are allowed to go there until the wedding ceremony *(perhaps the term wedding ceremony isn't the correct theological term but to me it encompasses the spirit of the occurrence)* between Jesus Christ and the redeemed takes place.

> And I heard as it were the voice of a great multitude, and as the voice of

many waters, and as the voice of mighty thunderings, saying, Alleluia: for the Lord God omnipotent reigneth.

Let us be glad and rejoice, and give honour to him: for the marriage of the Lamb is come, and his wife hath made herself ready.

And to her was granted that she should be arrayed in fine linen, clean and white: for the fine linen is the righteousness of saints.

And he saith unto me, Write, Blessed are they which are called unto the marriage supper of the Lamb. And he saith unto me, These are the true sayings of God...

And I saw a new heaven and a new earth: for the first heaven and the first earth were passed away; and there was no more sea.

And I John saw the holy city, new Jerusalem, coming down from God out of heaven, prepared as a bride adorned for her husband.

And I heard a great voice out of heaven saying, Behold, the tabernacle of God is with men, and he will dwell with them, and they shall be his people, and God himself shall be with them, and be their God.

And God shall wipe away all tears from their eyes; and there shall be no more death, neither sorrow, nor crying, neither shall there be any more pain: for the former things are passed away.

And he that sat upon the throne said, Behold, I make all things new. And he said unto me, Write: for these words are true and faithful.

And he said unto me, It is done. I am Alpha and Omega, the beginning and the end. I will give unto him that is athirst of the fountain of the water of life freely.

He that overcometh shall inherit all things; and I will be his God, and he shall be my son.

But the fearful, and unbelieving, and the abominable, and murderers, and whoremongers, and sorcerers, and idolaters, and all liars, shall have their part in the lake which burneth with fire and brimstone: which is the second death.

And there came unto me one of the seven angels which had the seven vials full of the seven last plagues, and talked with me, saying, Come hither, I will shew thee the bride, the Lamb's wife.

And he carried me away in the spirit to a great and high mountain, and shewed me that great city, the holy Jerusalem, descending out of heaven from God.

Revelation 19:6–9, 21:1–10 (KJV)

One evening after everyone had gone to bed, I prayed and told God that I wasn't going to work on this manuscript for a few weeks or maybe not at all. My plans were to leave the manuscript alone and go into my woodworking shop and make a piece of furniture or something that would please me. The next day, Saturday morning, it felt good to be back in my shop. After about an hour and a half in the shop, I noticed an air line needed to be moved. A simple matter of taking one step up onto a stepladder and attaching a hook in the ceiling and hanging the hose over that hook became God's moment to send me out of the shop and back to the manuscript. When I placed my right foot on the first step of the stepladder, a task I had successfully accomplished many times in the past, and began to raise myself up, it felt as though someone had shoved me. I had a good grip on the ladder and a good grip on a shelf bracket attached to the wall. My footing was exactly where it should have been, and I knew what I was doing. Holding on really tight, when I felt the shoving, I tightened my grip even more so I didn't go to the floor. The shoving feeling was very noticeable and troubling. Stabilizing myself and making sure I was in the correct position and my grip was firm, I began to go up the ladder again onto the first step. There was another shove. I held on tighter, and then there was another shove, and the ladder and I went to the floor. Somehow, and I cannot figure out how, the foot that wasn't even on the ladder or even touching the ladder received a broken toe next to the big toe. The fracture wasn't a simple fracture or break but a very serious break that required hospital treatment.

As I was preparing to leave, the hospital and the physician gave me some instructions. Stay off my foot for at least one week and use crutches and canes for the next four to six weeks otherwise the break wouldn't heal properly because the bone wasn't simply fractured; it was broken. What was I to do? Did God immobilize me so I couldn't do anything except sit around, watch TV, read a book, or sleep? Could it have been nothing more than a freak accident? Was I disoriented and didn't realize I was in an unsafe condition? Of course, all kinds of arguments or excuses could be made.

My wife drove me home, helped me into the house and to the couch, and there I stayed until bedtime. In bed, after my wife had gone to sleep, I looked toward heaven and prayed asking for an explanation for the accident. Immediately the impression came to me that I am now immobilized and that I must finish the manuscript. When I told a friend, who was acting as critic, and before I got to the part about going to the hospital, he stopped me and said, *I guess you got the message, huh.*

When I began working on the last chapter of the book, God said to me, "Remember Nineveh." Not understanding what God meant by remember Nineveh, I picked up a Bible and read the book of Jonah. The book of Jonah takes about ten to fifteen minutes to read.

We all know the story about Jonah and the whale and that God was going to destroy Nineveh. Jonah ran away in the opposite direction, thrown off the boat into the water, eaten by a big fish, vomited onto the shore wherein he wasted no time getting to Nineveh to deliver the message God had told him to deliver. Okay, I get all of that, and I understand. I was resisting what heaven wanted me to do and I suppose the broken toe was my big fish. I don't know but just maybe it was.

Whether you accept anything as fact or not, isn't important. Accepting, rejecting, believing, or not believing doesn't change whether anything is real or not. If it's real, it's real, and if it isn't, it isn't real, and our beliefs cannot make it real or unreal, nor change its existence. Since I was in paradise, I know it is real, and even if I hadn't been in paradise, I wouldn't take the chance of rejecting that which could be real. My mom always said an ounce of prevention is worth a pound of cure.

There is a spiritual battle that has been raging between Lucifer, that old Satan, and the Holy Trinity for many millennia. It is the evil that Lucifer offers that encourages millions of people to depart from righteousness. You might say that humanity is caught in the middle of the spiritual conflict. The good part is when God judged Adam and Eve for their disobedience, he gave humanity the free will to change our individual after-death destination. By default, thanks to Adam, we are now born destined to spend eternity with Lucifer, not God. We must make a conscious decision to change our destination. Humanity has an opportunity to make a choice. We can choose the offer from Jesus Christ, that is, accept Him as the Son of God, repent and seek redemption, and follow him or, by default, follow Lucifer. The sex, violence, dishonesty, murder, and it goes on and on, that is in this world must be vanquished. The only way to vanquish evil is to vanquish Lucifer.

There is no greater feeling than to be in an atmosphere completely void of evil. I know what that feels like because I have been there. If you listen to the theologians and religious scholars, they will tell you that in the end Satan will be bound for one thousand years then loosened for a little while, after which he will be cast into a lake of fire with his followers forever. Its only when he's cast in the lake of fire that evil will finally be removed from earth.

When Jonah delivered the message from God, the king proclaimed the message and the city repented. Individually each citizen and the leaders repented and the city was spared destruction. The message of Nineveh is when you hear the message, use the opportunity to repent individually, and choose to avoid the terrible things to come. Salvation, redemption, entry into paradise, and then into heaven is a personal act by one individual alone.

God will relieve humanity of things that are to come if all humanity repents and rids itself from evil, but they won't, and that is the problem. What humanity won't end, God must end.

Lamenting over when the terrible times will come as I witnessed in the visions shown to me in paradise, I sat down, and instead of my King James Version of the Bible, I picked up a book my wife had purchased many years ago called *The*

Book. *The Book* is the Bible written in modern-day language for ease of understanding. When I am seeking guidance from God, I will sometimes open my Bible at random, hoping God will give me the answer to my question. This time the Bible (*The Book*) opened to 2 Chronicles, chapter 34, starting with verse 14. The story is about Hilkiah the high priest. Hilkiah was recording the money collected at the Lord's temple. While doing so, he found the Book of the Law of the Lord scroll as it had been given through Moses. When the scroll had been read to the king, he tore his clothes in despair. The king sent Hilkiah and others to the newer section of Jerusalem to consult with the prophet Huldah. It turns out the prophet Huldah is a woman. She was the wife of Shallum, son of Tikvah, and grandson of Harhas, the keeper of the temple wardrobe. That struck me as odd because I have heard so often how women should be silent, and of what I have heard, there are religions that forbid women to participate with men. After reading 2 Chronicles, chapter 34 in "The Book" I went to my King James to see what it had to say.

Huldah said to them in 2 Chronicles 34:23–25 (KJV):

> And she answered them, Thus saith the LORD God of Israel, Tell ye the man that sent you to me,
>
> Thus saith the LORD, Behold, I will bring evil upon this place, and upon the inhabitants thereof, even all the curses that are written in the book which they have read before the king of Judah:
>
> Because they have forsaken me, and have burned incense unto other gods, that they might provoke me to anger with all the works of their hands; therefore my wrath shall be poured out upon this place, and shall not be quenched.

When God's sayings were reported back to the king, he humbled himself, tore his clothing, and wept before God in repentance.

> Because thine heart was tender, and thou didst humble thyself before God, when thou heardest his words against this place, and against the inhabitants thereof, and humbledst thyself before me, and didst rend thy clothes, and weep before me; I have even heard thee also, saith the LORD.
>
> Behold, I will gather thee to thy fathers, and thou shalt be gathered to thy grave in peace, neither shall thine eyes see all the evil that I will bring upon this place, and upon the inhabitants of the same. So they brought the king word again.
>
> 2 Chronicles 34:27–28 (KJV)

After reading these words, I was convinced God sent me to these writings as a personal message to confirm to me the time frame for the beginning of things to come.

Therefore, those things which are spoken about in John's Revelation and in Peter's Apocalypse must take place. Much of humanity will or already have humbled themselves. Because the kings, presidents, dictators, and leaders of the world won't humble themselves and lead the peoples of the world to follow, humanity is doomed. All except for those removed by, what some theologians call, the rapture. Humanity will be given another chance; some will choose to follow God; some won't. Those that don't will even hate God more and blame it all on him because they think he is a horrible God. That self-centered attitude by some of humanity is bringing on the need for God to rid earth and humanity of evil.

After God made Adam and Eve, he gave them one simple rule: Don't to eat the fruit from the tree of knowledge.

And the LORD God commanded the man, saying, Of every tree of the garden thou mayest freely eat:

But of the tree of the knowledge of good and evil, thou shalt not eat of it: for in the day that thou eatest thereof thou shalt surely die.

Genesis 2:16–17 (KJV)

The most important gift and responsibility God gave to Adam and humanity is the free will to govern or not govern in a righteous manner. Except for the governing rules God placed in our mind and hearts, I could find no other rules mentioned in the Bible at creation. Humanity was required to use the God-given inner rules to control their actions and to remain righteous. There were no lawyers, courts, judges, jails, or executioners to issue punishment for failing to follow righteousness.

When Cain killed Abel, God marked him and vanquished him to be a vagabond for the remainder of his life.

If thou doest well, shalt thou not be accepted? and if thou doest not well, sin lieth at the door. And unto thee shall be his desire, and thou shalt rule over him.

And Cain talked with Abel his brother: and it came to pass, when they were in the field, that Cain rose up against Abel his brother, and slew him.

And the LORD said unto Cain, Where is Abel thy brother? And he said, I know not: Am I my brother's keeper?

And he said, What hast thou done? the voice of thy brother's blood crieth unto me from the ground.

And now art thou cursed from the earth, which hath opened her mouth to receive thy brother's blood from thy hand;

When thou tillest the ground, it shall not henceforth yield unto thee her strength; a fugitive and a vagabond shalt thou be in the earth.

And Cain said unto the LORD, My punishment is greater than I can bear.

Behold, thou hast driven me out this day from the face of the earth; and from thy face shall I be hid; and I shall be a fugitive and a vagabond in the earth; and it shall come to pass, that every one that findeth me shall slay me.

And the LORD said unto him, Therefore whosoever slayeth Cain, vengeance shall be taken on him sevenfold. And the LORD set a mark upon Cain, lest any finding him should kill him.

Genesis 4:7–16 (KJV)

Why is it we cannot govern ourselves with righteousness? God also gave man the power of dominion over every living thing. Along with dominion, he gave man absolute responsibility for the care taking of his earth and creations. Genesis 1:26:

> And God said, Let us make man in our image, after our likeness: and let them have dominion over the fish of the sea, and over the fowl of the air, and over the cattle, and over all the earth, and over every creeping thing that creepeth upon the earth.

When man did good, he received credit, but when he did badly, he received the blame. Humanity won't accept blame or responsibility; rather, we try to blame God or someone else for everything that goes wrong. The most powerful gift we possess is the ability to make good or bad decisions. Unfortunately, Lucifer has convinced a great portion of humanity that personal pleasures are more important than righteousness and responsibility, and it all began in the Garden of Eden. Genesis 3:1–7:

Now the serpent was more subtle than any beast of the field which the LORD God had made. And he said unto the woman, Yea, hath God said, Ye shall not eat of every tree of the garden?

And the woman said unto the serpent, We may eat of the fruit of the trees of the garden:

But of the fruit of the tree which is in the midst of the garden, God hath said, Ye shall not eat of it, neither shall ye touch it, lest ye die.

And the serpent said unto the woman, Ye shall not surely die:

For God doth know that in the day ye eat thereof, then your eyes shall be opened, and ye shall be as gods, knowing good and evil.

And when the woman saw that the tree was good for food, and that it was pleasant to the eyes, and a tree to be desired to make one wise, she took of the fruit thereof, and did eat, and gave also unto her husband with her; and he did eat.

And the eyes of them both were opened, and they knew that they were naked; and they sewed fig leaves together, and made themselves aprons.

Unlike humanity, when God gives his word, it is forever and irrevocable. When Adam and Eve gave their word not to eat the fruit then failed to keep their word, the blame game began. Wasn't Adam, instead of taking responsibility as he should have for the actions of his mate, blamed her for his weakness? Genesis 3:12–13:

And the man said, The woman whom thou gavest to be with me, she gave me of the tree, and I did eat.

And the Lord God said unto the woman, What is this that thou hast done? And the woman said, The serpent beguiled me, and I did eat.

God made Eve to be a companion and helpmate to Adam, but Adam was never relieved of the ultimate responsibility for her actions. Genesis 3:17:

> And unto Adam he said, Because thou hast hearkened unto the voice of thy wife, and hast eaten of the tree, of which I commanded thee, saying, Thou shalt not eat of it: cursed is the ground for thy sake; in sorrow shalt thou eat of it all the days of thy life.

The serpent, often called Satan, but who in reality is Lucifer, the great deceiver, worked on Adam's companion as he works on our peers, friends and loved ones to entice us to participate in evil.

Are we being deceived by Lucifer? Of course we are, and it's not going to get any better. When the subject of righteousness or religion comes up most people want to know what religion is good and what religion is bad. Rather than trying to determine which religion is bad or good doesn't it make more sense to ask which one works, and are there any witnesses? I know very little of other religions and quite frankly I don't care because I've been to paradise, I've seen Jesus, I've interacted with angels and I know they're awaiting my return. Time is running out! Luke 21:20–36:

> And when ye shall see Jerusalem compassed with armies, then know that the desolation thereof is nigh.
>
> Then let them which are in Judaea flee to the mountains; and let them which are in the midst of it depart out; and let not them that are in the countries enter thereinto.
>
> For these be the days of vengeance, that all things which are written may be fulfilled.

But woe unto them that are with child, and to them that give suck, in those days! for there shall be great distress in the land, and wrath upon this people.

And they shall fall by the edge of the sword, and shall be led away captive into all nations: and Jerusalem shall be trodden down of the Gentiles, until the times of the Gentiles be fulfilled.

And there shall be signs in the sun, and in the moon, and in the stars; and upon the earth distress of nations, with perplexity; the sea and the waves roaring;

Men's hearts failing them for fear, and for looking after those things which are coming on the earth: for the powers of heaven shall be shaken.

And then shall they see the Son of man coming in a cloud with power and great glory.

And when these things begin to come to pass, then look up, and lift up your heads; for your redemption draweth nigh.

And he spake to them a parable; Behold the fig tree, and all the trees;

When they now shoot forth, ye see and know of your own selves that summer is now nigh at hand.

So likewise ye, when ye see these things come to pass, know ye that the kingdom of God is nigh at hand.

Verily I say unto you, This generation shall not pass away, till all be fulfilled.

Heaven and earth shall pass away: but my words shall not pass away.

And take heed to yourselves, lest at any time your hearts be overcharged with surfeiting, and drunkenness, and cares of this life, and so that day come upon you unawares.

For as a snare shall it come on all them that dwell on the face of the whole earth.

Watch ye therefore, and pray always, that ye may be accounted worthy to escape all these things that shall come to pass, and to stand before the Son of man.

Consider the possibility—just perhaps God allowed me to see all that I saw because he knew or was preparing me to write these things at this particular moment in time. Don't get me wrong, I'm not saying that is the case or I'm not saying that was not the case, I'm simply saying: consider the possibility. When I have prayed asking God how I should respond to anyone asking me why I wrote these things, my response must always be the same—Tell them this is the final warning.